Daily Math
Warm-Ups
Grade Two

by
M.J. Owen

Carson-Dellosa Publishing Company, Inc.
Greensboro, North Carolina

Credits

Editors
Hank Rudisill
Amy Gamble

Cover Design
Dez Perrotti

Cover Photo
EyeWire Images

Layout Design
Hank Rudisill

Art Coordinator
Betsy Peninger

Artist
Jon Nawrocik

ISBN 0-88724-818-7

Table of Contents
Daily Math Warm-Ups Grade Two

Introduction to *Daily Math Warm-Ups*

Based on standards specified by the National Council of Teachers of Mathematics (NCTM), *Daily Math Warm-Ups* will give teachers a year-long collection of challenging problems that reinforce math skills taught in the classroom. Designed around the traditional school year, the series offers 180 daily lessons (sets of five problems each) including computation, graph, and word problems. For each two-week group of lessons, an eight-problem multiple-choice assessment is provided to help you easily identify which students have mastered which concepts. The daily practice will help improve students' skills and bolster their confidence.

How to Use This Book

You can use this book in the following ways:
- Use the problems as a daily math warm-up. Make each child responsible for keeping a math journal which is checked periodically. Copy the daily lessons on transparencies. At the beginning of each class, put the problems on an overhead and give students approximately five minutes to solve the problems. When students have completed the exercise, go over the problems as a class. You can use this opportunity to discuss why some answers are correct and others are not.
- Because copying from the board or overhead is challenging for some learners, you may choose to photocopy the daily lessons for particular students, or for the entire class. Have students work on the problems at the beginning of class, then continue as described above.
- Give each student a copy of the problems near the end of class and have them turn the work in as a "Ticket Out the Door." You can then check students' work and then return their work and go over the answers at the beginning of the next class period.

Daily Math Warm-Ups includes many elements that will help students master a wide range of mathematical concepts. These include:

- 180 five-problem lessons based on standards specified by the National Council of Teachers of Mathematics

- 18 multiple-choice assessment tests in standardized-test format, to help identify concepts mastered and concepts in need of reteaching

- 12 real-world application extension activities

- A reproducible problem-solving strategy guide for students (on the inside back cover)

- Plenty of computation, graph, and word-problem solving opportunities that become more difficult as students progress through the school year

Lesson 1

1. Look at the Base Ten Blocks. Write the number shown.

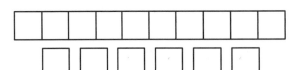

_____

2. $5 + 2 =$

3. $5 - 2 =$

4. $2 + 3 =$

5. Write a number sentence and solve the problem. Leo had 6 goldfish. He gave away 2 goldfish. How many goldfish does Leo have left?

_____

Leo has _____ goldfish left.

Lesson 2

1. Peter ate 4 grapes. Later, he ate 3 more grapes. How many grapes did Peter eat in all?

Peter ate _____ grapes in all.

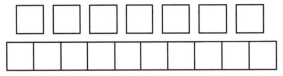

2. $3 + 6 =$

3. $4 - 3 =$

4. $1 + 7 =$

5. Look at the Base Ten Blocks. Cross out 7 blocks. Complete the number sentence and solve the problem.

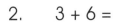 $- 7 =$ _____

5

Lesson 3

1. Write the number. 1 ten, 9 ones _____

2. 6 + 5 =

3. 7 – 2 =

4. Write a number sentence and solve the problem. The teacher has a cup with 5 pens in it. If 3 pens do not work, how many pens work?

    _____

    _____ pens work.

5. Write the number sixteen. _____

Lesson 4

1. Write a number sentence and solve the problem. There are 6 triangles drawn on a piece of paper. If 2 triangles are erased, how many triangles are left?

    _____

    _____ triangles are left.

2. Count by 2s. 2, 4, _____, _____, 10, _____

3. 6 + 3 =

4. 7 + 3 =

5. Look at the Base Ten Blocks. Write the number shown.

    _____

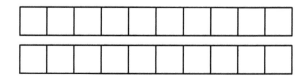

Lesson 5

1. Write the number. 1 ten, 4 ones _____

2. Write a number sentence and solve the problem. In Becky's art class, there are 2 boys and 3 girls. How many boys and girls are in Becky's art class altogether?

   _____

   There are _____ boys and girls in Becky's art class altogether.

3. $4 + 4 =$

4. $6 - 4 =$

5. In the box, draw Base Ten Blocks to show the number 20.

Lesson 6

1. $2 + 8 =$

2. $8 + 4 =$

3. $8 - 6 =$

4. Write the number eighteen. _____

5. Write a number sentence and solve the problem. There are 7 baseballs and 6 basketballs in the sports closet. How many baseballs and basketballs are there in all?

   _____

   There are _____ baseballs and basketballs in all.

Lesson 7

1. The phone rings 9 times in 1 hour. The next hour, the phone rings 7 times. How many times does the phone ring in all?

   The phone rings _____ times in all.

2. $4 + 5 =$

3. $9 - 6 =$

4. $8 - 5 =$

5. Put the numbers in order from least to greatest. 6, 4, 16, 12, 11

   _____, _____, _____, _____, _____

Lesson 8

1. $4 + 5 =$

2. Write a number sentence and solve the problem. Kelly has 6 bananas in her cart. She adds 4 more bananas. How many bananas are in Kelly's cart now?

   _____

   Kelly has _____ bananas in her cart.

3. $9 - 8 =$

4. Write the number. 1 ten, 7 ones _____

5. Look at the Base Ten Blocks.
   Write the number shown.

   _____

8

Lesson 9

1. Look at the number in the box. Circle the number in the tens place. Cross out the number in the ones place.

   18

2. Write a number sentence and solve the problem. Jake is driving to the mall. The mall is 5 miles from Jake's house. After he travels 3 miles, he stops at a gas station. How many more miles does Jake have to travel?

   _____

   Jake has to travel _____ more miles.

3. $9 + 1 =$

4. $7 - 6 =$

5. Write the numbers in order from least to greatest. 7, 10, 14, 15, 2

   _____, _____, _____, _____, _____

Lesson 10

1. Write a number sentence and solve the problem. Andrea buys a box of 9 ice pops. If 7 ice pops are orange and the rest are purple, how many ice pops are purple?

   _____

   _____ ice pops are purple.

2. $8 + 7 =$

3. $6 + 5 =$

4. $8 - 4 =$

5. Put the numbers in order from greatest to least. 5, 9, 17, 3, 13

   _____, _____, _____, _____, _____

Lesson 11

1. J.J. has 15 coins in his collection. He gives away 4 coins. How many coins does J.J. have left?

    J.J. has _____ coins left.

2. 11 + 1 =

3. 10 − 6 =

4. 10 + 8 =

5. Look at the picture. Write the number sentence that the picture shows. Then, solve the problem.

    _____

Lesson 12

1. Draw the missing shape to complete the pattern.

      _____

2. Write a number sentence and solve the problem. There are 12 books on one shelf and 5 books on a second shelf. How many books are there in all?

    _____

    There are _____ books in all.

3. 12 + 4 =

4. Count by 2s. 10, 12, 14, _____, 18, 20, _____

5. 11 − 5 =

Lesson 13

1. Write a number sentence and solve the problem. Chandra bakes 12 cookies. She burns 9 cookies. How many cookies are not burned?

   _____

   _____ cookies are not burned.

2. $12 + 6 =$

3. $9 - 7 =$

4. $12 + 3 =$

5. In the box, draw a picture to show the number sentence $4 - 2 =$.

Lesson 14

1. Write a number sentence and solve the problem. Peter buys 11 balloons. If 2 balloons pop, how many balloons does Peter have left?

   _____

   Peter has _____ balloons left.

2. $10 + 9 =$

3. Count by 2s. 16, 18, 20, _____, 24, _____, 28

4. $10 + 6 =$

5. $5 + 9 =$

Lesson 15

1. There are 12 students in Maggie's class. If 7 students live in Maggie's neighborhood and the rest of the students live in another neighborhood, how many students live in another neighborhood?

   _____ students live in another neighborhood.

2. In the box, draw a picture to show the number sentence $10 - 4 =$.

3. $8 - 8 =$

4. $9 + \_\_\_\_ = 17$

5. $11 + 9 =$

Lesson 16

1. The mail carrier delivers 7 letters. If 1 of the letters has the wrong zip code on it, how many of the letters have the correct zip code?

   _____ letters have the correct zip code.

2. $12 - 2 =$

3. $11 + 7 =$

4. $6 + 9 =$

5. Write the missing letters to complete the pattern.

   M, M, N, O, O, P, Q, Q, _____, S, S, _____

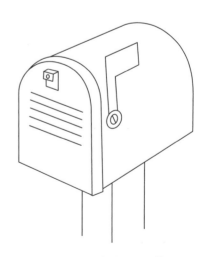

Lesson 17

1. Mark bought ice cream cones for his family and friends. He bought 11 chocolate cones and 7 vanilla cones. How many chocolate and vanilla cones did Mark buy in all?

   Mark bought _____ chocolate and vanilla cones in all.

2. Draw a picture in the box to show the number sentence $4 + 6 =$.

3. $12 + 8 =$

4. $6 + $ _____ $= 12$

5. $11 + 7 =$

Lesson 18

1. $11 + 5 =$

2. $11 - 5 =$

3. _____ $+ 8 = 10$

4. Mary read 11 books on Monday and 7 books on Tuesday. How many more books did Mary read on Monday?

   Mary read _____ more books on Monday.

5. Look at the picture. Write the number sentence that the picture shows. Then, solve the problem.

Lesson 19

1. Count by 5s. 5, 10, 15, 20, _____, _____, 35, 40

2. James buys 6 nails and 3 hammers at the hardware store. How many more nails than hammers did James buy at the hardware store?

    James bought _____ more nails than hammers at the hardware store.

3. Look at the picture. Write the number sentence that the picture shows. Then, solve the problem.

    _____

4. 13 + 2 =

5. 19 − 3 =

Lesson 20

1. 9 + 11 =

2. 12 − 4 =

3. 12 + 4 =

4. Write a number sentence and solve the problem. There are 7 children swimming in a pool. If 3 children get out of the pool, how many children are still in the pool?

    _____

    _____ children are still in the pool.

5. Draw the missing shape to complete the pattern.

Name _____

Lesson 21

1. Look at the picture graph. How many students have names that begin with P?

   _____ students have names that begin with P.

2. $18 - 8 =$

3. $10 - 0 =$

4. _____ $+ 4 = 10$

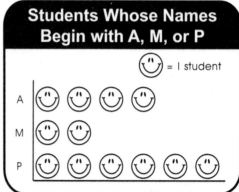

Students Whose Names Begin with A, M, or P

😊 = 1 student

A 😊 😊 😊 😊
M 😊 😊
P 😊 😊 😊 😊 😊 😊

5. Write a number sentence and solve the problem. On Monday, Jessica ironed 5 blue shirts and 6 white shirts. How many shirts did she iron in all?

   _____

   Jessica ironed _____ shirts in all.

Lesson 22

1. Look at the bar graph. How many children voted for watermelon as their favorite fruit?

   _____ children voted for watermelon.

2. $17 + 1 =$

3. $18 - 6 =$

4. $14 - 2 =$

Favorite Fruit

Number of Children

Type of Fruit: Watermelon, Pear, Apple, Orange, Grapes

5. Mr. Callaway ordered 17 pizzas for lunch on field day. If 6 pizzas have pepperoni on them and the rest have sausage, how many pizzas have sausage on them?

   _____ pizzas have sausage on them.

Name _____

Lesson 23

1. _____ + 8 = 11

2. 15 – 3 =

3. 17 – 4 =

4. Look at the picture graph. How many phone calls did Melissa receive on Monday and Tuesday?

    Melissa received _____ phone calls on Monday and Tuesday.

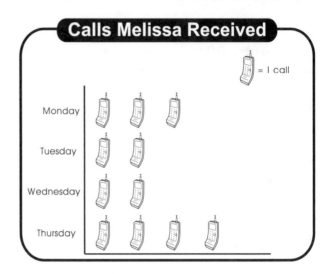

Calls Melissa Received

= 1 call

Monday
Tuesday
Wednesday
Thursday

5. Ted has 14 tennis balls. He loses 4 tennis balls. How many tennis balls does Ted have now?

    Ted has _____ tennis balls now.

Lesson 24

1. Look at the bar graph. How many more pictures did Mr. Jewels take on vacation than at the wedding?

    Mr. Jewels took _____ more pictures on vacation than at the wedding.

2. Count by 5s. 25, 30, 35, _____, _____, 50

3. 15 + 5 =

4. 4 + _____ = 7

Pictures Mr. Jewels Took

Number of Pictures

16
15
14
13
12
11
10
9
8
7
6
5
4
3
2
1
0

Wedding   Vacation   Picnic   Baseball

Event

5. Kelsey has 17 color photos and 6 black-and-white photos that she wants to put in an album. How many more color photos does Kelsey have than black-and-white photos?

    Kelsey has _____ more color photos.

Lesson 25

1. Look at the picture graph. How many days had temperatures above 100°F during June, July, and August total?

   _____ days had temperatures above 100°F during June, July, and August.

2. $13 + 13 =$

3. $9 - 9 =$

4. $15 - 2 =$

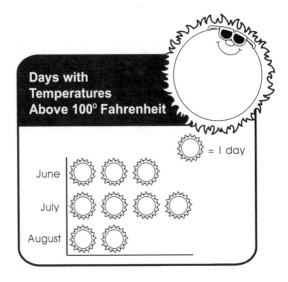

Days with Temperatures Above 100° Fahrenheit

= 1 day

June

July

August

5. Hannah is playing a game with buttons. She starts with 15 buttons. She wins 12 more buttons. How many buttons does Hannah have at the end of the game?

   Hannah has _____ buttons at the end of the game.

Lesson 26

1. Look at the tally chart. Based on the chart, which winter activity is the most popular?

   _____ is the most popular winter activity.

2. There are 4 boys in line. Ken is third in line. How many boys are behind Ken in line?

   _____ boy is behind Ken in line.

3. $8 + 9 =$

4. $16 - 10 =$

5. $18 + 12 =$

Favorite Winter Activity

Skiing	Ice Skating
‖‖‖ ‖‖‖	‖‖‖ |||
Sledding	Hockey
‖‖‖	‖‖‖ ‖‖‖	

Lesson 27

1. Look at the picture graph. How many sandwiches were ordered at Avenue B Deli in all?

   _____ sandwiches were ordered at Avenue B Deli in all.

Sandwiches Ordered at Avenue B Deli

= 2 sandwiches

Turkey

Ham

Tuna

Chicken Salad

2. 14 + 15 =

3. 17 − 6 =

4. 14 − 3 =

5. Tim invited 3 friends to go swimming. If 1 of his friends forgot his towel, how many of Tim's friends remembered their towels?

   _____ of Tim's friends remembered their towels.

Lesson 28

1. Look at the tally chart. How many more boys than girls attended the talent show?

   _____ more boys than girls attended the talent show.

Talent Show Attendance

Boys	Girls
ﬀﬀ ﬀﬀ ﬀﬀ |||	ﬀﬀ ﬀﬀ ﬀﬀ

2. 10 + 18 =

3. 18 + 20 =

4. 30 − 10 =

5. Jeff takes a container of 17 marbles to the park. On the way to the park, he spills the container and loses 12 marbles. How many marbles does Jeff have now?

   Jeff has _____ marbles now.

Lesson 29

1. A group of 12 friends order lunch. If 5 friends order hot dogs and the rest of the friends order hamburgers, how many friends order hamburgers?

   _____ friends order hamburgers.

2. Count by 10s. 10, 20, _____, _____, 50, 60

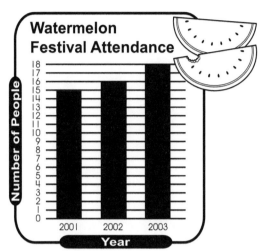

3. 10 + 29 =

4. 18 − 9 =

5. Look at the bar graph. Based on the bar graph, circle the letter beside the statement below that is true.

   A. Attendance at the Watermelon Festival has increased every year.
   B. Attendance at the Watermelon Festival has decreased every year.
   C. Attendance at the Watermelon Festival has been the same every year.
   D. There is not enough information in the graph to answer the question.

Lesson 30

1. If 7 dogs are final contestants in the annual Bark-a-Thon, and only 1 dog wins first place, how many dogs do not win first place?

   _____ dogs do not win first place.

2. 13 − 8 =

3. 25 − 14 =

4. 15 + 15 =

Students' Favorite Seasons			
Winter	Spring	Summer	Fall
﹢﹢﹢﹢ ﹢﹢﹢﹢ ﹢﹢﹢﹢	||	﹢﹢﹢﹢ |||	﹢﹢﹢﹢	﹢﹢﹢﹢

5. Look at the tally chart. How many students like winter better than spring?

   _____ students like winter better than spring.

Lesson 31

1. If 18 birds are resting in a tree and 7 birds are chirping, how many birds are not chirping?

    _____ birds are not chirping.

2. Circle the even number.   2   5   7

3. $18 - 11 =$

4. $15 + 12 =$

5. Look at the bar graph. How many students voted for cookies or fruit as their favorite snack?

    _____ nts voted for cookies or fruit orite snack.

Favorite Snack

(bar graph: Times Favored vs. Snack Food — Chips 5, Cookies 9, Fruit 7, Pretzel 11)

Lesson 32

1. _____ dd number.   8   10   7

2. $14 - 10 =$

3. $14 + 10 =$

4. Look at the table. How many more pencils than red pens do second graders need to bring to school?

    Second graders need to bring _____ more pencils than red pens.

Grade 2 Supplies	
Supply	**Number Needed**
Pencils	18
Red Pens	2
Notebooks	6
Journals	2
Crayons	2
Scissors	1
Glue	3

5. Pam spent 7 hours at the park on Saturday. On Sunday, she spent 8 hours at the park. How many hours did Pam spend at the park all weekend?

    Pam spent _____ hours at the park all weekend.

Lesson 33

1. Look at the picture graph. How many puppies did Fifi, Princess, and Charm have altogether?

   Fifi, Princess, and Charm had a total of _____ puppies.

Number of Puppies in a Litter

🦴 = I puppy

Fifi	🦴 🦴 🦴
Princess	🦴 🦴 🦴 🦴
Charm	🦴 🦴 🦴 🦴 🦴 🦴

2. Jay decorated 15 chocolate cupcakes and 4 vanilla cupcakes. How many more chocolate cupcakes did Jay decorate?

   Jay decorated _____ more chocolate cupcakes.

3. 17 + 8 =

4. 16 + 11 =

5. 20 − 0 =

Lesson 34

1. Meg has 16 mints in her pocket. She g_____ts. How many mints does Meg have now?

   Meg has _____ mints now.

2. Count by 10s. 50, 60, _____, 80, 90, _____

3. 14 − 12 =

4. 6 + 16 =

5. Look at the tally chart. How many more babies weighed 7 pounds than weighed 9 pounds?

   _____ more babies weighed 7 pounds than weighed 9 pounds.

Birth Weights

6 Pounds	7 Pounds
IIII	⊬⊬⊬
8 Pounds	**9 Pounds**
IIII	III

Lesson 35

1. Circle the even number.   22   25   15   9

2. 15 + 15 =

3. 12 − 10 =

4. How many total elm, oak, and ash trees are in Hannah's yard?

    There are _____ total elm, oak, and ash trees in Hannah's yard.

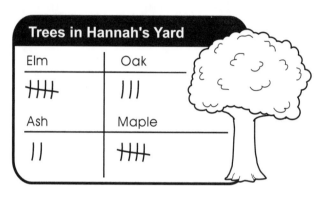

Trees in Hannah's Yard

Elm	Oak
$\cancel{||||}$	|||
Ash	Maple
||	$\cancel{||||}$

5. Miguel has 18 pairs of shorts in his closet. He also has 12 shirts in his closet. How ~~many~~ ...othing does Miguel have in his closet in all?

    Miguel has _____ ...thing in his closet in all.

Lesson 36

I for Shayla

1. 13 + 8 =

2. 14 + 9 =

3. 16 − 5 =

4. Look at the bar graph. How many people attended the fair on Saturday or Sunday?

    _____ people attended the fair on Saturday or Sunday.

5. Look at the Base Ten Blocks. Write the number shown.

    _____

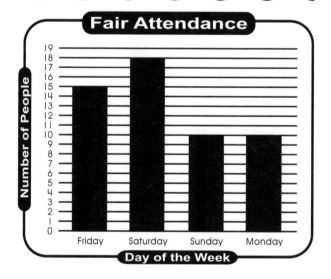

Fair Attendance

Number of People / Day of the Week

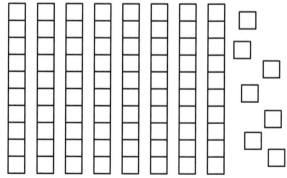

Lesson 37

1. 17 − 11 =

2. 15 + 7 =

3. 38 + 10 =

Fruit Mr. Hatley Bought at the Store

Fruit	Pounds
Bananas	4
Apples	3
Peaches	4
Strawberries	2
Plums	6

4. Look at the chart. How many pounds of peaches, strawberries, and plums did Mr. Hatley buy?

    Mr. Hatley bought _____ pounds of peaches, strawberries, and plums.

5. Julie has 16 red balls and 14 blue balls. How many balls does she have in all?

    Julie has _____ balls in all.

Lesson 38

1. Look at the picture graph. How many more eggs were laid on Thursday and Friday than on Saturday and Sunday?

    _____ more eggs were laid on Thursday and Friday than on Saturday and Sunday.

2. Count by 5s. 75, 80, 85, _____, _____, 100

3. 24 + 15 =

4. Wendy is seventh in line waiting for a store to open. There are 17 people waiting in line. How many people are in line behind Wendy?

    _____ people are in line behind Wendy.

5. Look at the Base Ten Blocks. Write the number shown.

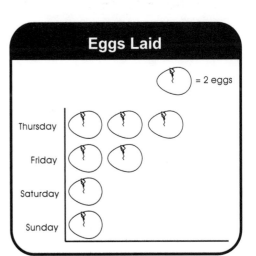

Eggs Laid

= 2 eggs

Thursday
Friday
Saturday
Sunday

Lesson 39

1. 74 + 23 =

2. 46 − 15 =

3. Circle the odd number.
    28   6   19   4

4. Write the number eighty-eight.

    _____

5. Maggie picks 28 flowers. Jenny picks 16 flowers. How many more flowers does Maggie pick than Jenny?

    Maggie picks _____ more flowers.

Lesson 40

1. 17 − 6 =

2. 17 + 3 =

3. Look at the tally chart. Which color was the most popular?

    _____ was the most popular color.

4. Write the number fifty-three.

    _____

5. Look at the Base Ten Blocks. Write the number shown.

    _____

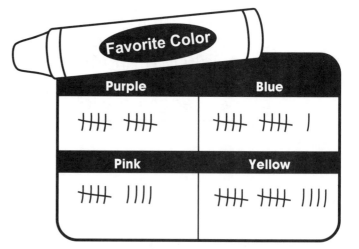

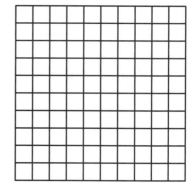

Lesson 41

1. A total of 17 goldfish are being given away as prizes at the school carnival. If 6 of the goldfish are orange and the rest are yellow, how many of the goldfish are yellow?

   _____ of the goldfish are yellow.

2. $12 + 7 =$

3. $15 +$ _____ $= 17$

4. $18 - 6 =$

5. Draw the missing rocks in the box to complete the pattern.

Lesson 42

1. $42 + 26 =$

2. Write the missing numbers to complete the pattern.

   45, 40, 35, 30, _____, _____, 15, 10

3. Dana's dog has 18 bones. Her dog buries 4 bones. How many bones does her dog have now?

   The dog has _____ bones.

4. $14 - 12 =$

5. Count by 10s.

   10, _____, _____, 40, 50, _____, _____, _____, _____, 100

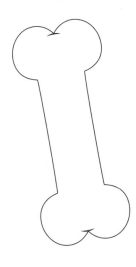

Lesson 43

1. 18 + 10 =

2. 10 − 0 =

3. 17 − 12 =

4. Draw the missing beans in the box to complete the pattern.

 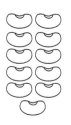 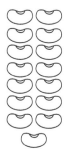  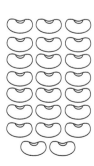

5. Mia spends 18 days at the beach. It rains 16 of the days that Mia is visiting the beach. How many days does it not rain?

    It does not rain _____ days while Mia is at the beach.

Lesson 44

1. Write the missing numbers to complete the pattern.

    5, 10, 15, _____, 25, _____, 35, 40

2. Joey is running a race that is 15 miles long. He stops to eat an energy bar after running 11 miles. How many miles does Joey have left to run?

    Joey has _____ miles left to run.

3. 23 + 22 =

4. 34 − 11 =

5. 76 − 51 =

Lesson 45

1. Shandra has 16 stickers. She buys 14 more stickers while she is on vacation. How many stickers does Shandra have now?

    Shandra has _____ stickers now.

2. $40 + 30 =$

3. $18 - 15 =$

4. $15 + 3 =$

5. Draw the missing buttons in the box to complete the pattern.

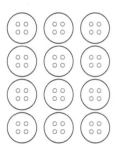 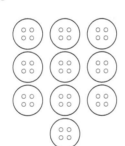 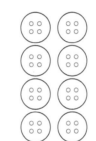  

Lesson 46

1. There are 12 campers in the lake for an afternoon swim. If 6 more campers join them, how many campers are in the lake in all?

    There are _____ campers in the lake in all.

2. $5 + \underline{\hspace{1cm}} = 12$

3. $88 - 77 =$

4. $\underline{\hspace{1cm}} + 9 = 12$

5. Write the missing letters to complete the pattern.

    J, A, K, A, L, A, M, A, _____, A, _____, A, P, A

Lesson 47

Name _____

1. Kayla rakes 14 piles of leaves in her front yard and 15 piles of leaves in her backyard. How many piles of leaves does Kayla rake in all?

    Kayla rakes _____ piles of leaves in all.

2. Circle the letter beside the statement that best describes what is happening in the pattern. 12, 10, 13, 11, 14, 12, 15, 13, 16, 14, 17

    A. First, 3 is added. Then, 2 is subtracted.
    B. First, 2 is subtracted. Then, 2 is added.
    C. First, 2 is subtracted. Then, 4 is added.
    D. First, 2 is subtracted. Then, 3 is added.

3. 16 + 22 =

4. 81 + 13 =

5. 52 + 10 =

Lesson 48

1. Write the name of each missing animal to complete the pattern.

2. There are 17 turtles and 9 rabbits in a race. If 4 turtles do not finish the race, how many turtles do finish the race?

    _____ turtles do finish the race.

3. 35 + 13 =

4. 74 + 3 =

5. 11 − 1 =

Lesson 49

1. 6 + 8 =

2. 10 + 10 + 10 =

3. 48 – 25 =

4. How many more fruits are there than vegetables?

       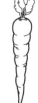

   There are _____ more fruits than vegetables.

5. At recess, 9 students are playing kickball. If 4 students playing hopscotch decide to play kickball instead, how many children are playing kickball now?

   _____ children are playing kickball now.

Lesson 50

1. Betsy's family must travel 58 miles to get to the beach. Before they arrive at the beach, they stop for lunch. Betsy's mom tells her that they only have to travel 21 more miles before they will arrive at the beach. How many miles has Betsy's family already traveled?

   Betsy's family has already traveled _____ miles.

2. 92 – 61 =

3. 15 – 12 =

4. 13 + 43 =

5. Write the missing letters to complete the pattern.

   A, D, G, _____, M, _____, S, V, Y

Lesson 51

1. Jill wrote 18 pages in her journal on Monday and 16 more pages on Tuesday. How many pages did Jill write on Monday and Tuesday together?

    Jill wrote _____ pages in her journal on Monday and Tuesday together.

2. Circle the best answer. About how long is a marker?

    10 centimeters   10 meters   10 miles

3. 17 + 15 =

4. 14 – 8 =

5. Circle the letter beside the number sentence that the picture shows.

    A. 3 + 4 = 7   B. 12 – 4 = 8

    C. 11 + 4 = 15   D. 11 – 4 = 7

Lesson 52

1. Round the number to the nearest tens place. 75 _____

2. Mrs. Pearson makes 20 cupcakes for her daughter's class. She puts sprinkles on 10 of the cupcakes. How many of the cupcakes does Mrs. Pearson not put sprinkles on?

    Mrs. Pearson does not put sprinkles on _____ cupcakes.

3. 15 – 8 =

4. 12 + 19 =

5. Fill in the blank with >, <, or = to make the number sentence true.

    43 _____ 14

Lesson 53

1. William attended swim class for 15 hours in June and 15 hours in July. How many hours total did William attend swimming lessons?

   William attended swimming lessons for _____ hours total.

2. Circle the letter beside the number sentence that the picture shows.

   A. $2 + 6 = 8$ B. $6 - 2 = 4$

   C. $6 + 3 = 9$ D. $6 - 3 = 3$

3. $18 + 17 =$

4. $16 - 9 =$

5. Use centimeters to measure the length of the paper clip.

   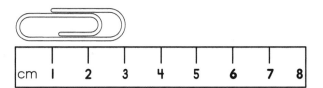

   The paper clip is _____ centimeters long.

Lesson 54

1. Rashad has 17 CDs in his music collection. James has 14 more CDs than Rashad. How many CDs does James have?

   James has a total of _____ CDs.

2. Round the number to the nearest tens place. 61 _____

3. $68 - 10 =$

4. $16 + 4 =$

5. Circle the letter beside the number sentence that the picture shows.

   A. $11 + 3 = 14$ B. $14 + 4 = 18$

   C. $13 + 3 = 16$ D. $12 - 4 = 8$

Lesson 55

1. Mr. and Ms. Russell have 9 grandchildren. If 7 of their grandchildren have red hair and the rest of their grandchildren have brown hair, how many of their grandchildren have brown hair?

    _____ of their grandchildren have brown hair.

2. Round the number to the nearest tens place. 44 _____

3. Fill in the blank with >, <, or = to make the number sentence true.

    22 _____ 22

4. $18 + 5 =$

5. $98 - 42 =$

Lesson 56

1. Round the number to the nearest tens place. 77 _____

2. $38 - 16 =$

3. Ann buys 10 bubble wands to give away as birthday presents. She gives away 7 bubble wands during the school year. How many bubble wands does Ann have left?

    Ann has _____ bubble wands left.

4. Use centimeters to measure the height of the glue bottle.

    The glue bottle is _____ centimeters high.

5. $13 + 9 =$

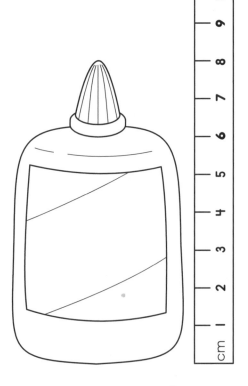

Lesson 57

1. Serena writes the numbers 17 and 16 on two cards. She asks her brother to add the numbers and write the total on another card. If he is correct, what number should Serena's brother write on the card?

   Serena's brother should write the number _____ on the card.

2. Write the number sentence that the picture shows. Then, solve the number sentence.

   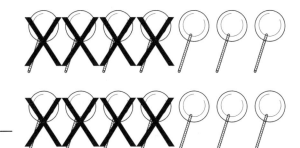

   _____

3. $15 + 16 =$

4. Round the number to the nearest tens place. 56 _____

5. Round the number to the nearest tens place. 12 _____

Lesson 58

1. Tim is putting together a wagon. The instruction book is 13 pages long. He has read the first 8 pages of the book. How many pages does Tim have left to read?

   Tim has _____ pages left to read.

2. $16 + 16 =$

3. $18 - 9 =$

4. $17 + 13 =$

5. Write the number sentence that the picture shows. Then, solve the number sentence.

   _____

Lesson 59

1. 75 – 44 =

2. 15 + 19 =

3. 15 + 8 =

4. LaKisha is making baskets of cookies for 16 of her neighbors. She puts chocolate chip cookies in 13 of the baskets. She puts oatmeal cookies in the rest of the baskets. How many baskets have oatmeal cookies?

    _____ baskets have oatmeal cookies.

5. Look at the picture. Write the number sentence that the picture shows. Then, solve the number sentence.

    _____

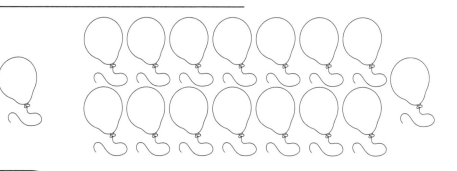

Lesson 60

1. 12 + 18 =

2. 17 – 8 =

3. 14 – 9 =

4. Round the number to the nearest tens place. 87 _____

5. Lily and John blew up balloons for the picnic. There were 3 red, 5 white, and 11 blue balloons. If 5 balloons popped before the picnic, how many balloons were left when the picnic started?

    _____ balloons were left when the picnic started.

Lesson 61

1. Circle the dog that has an odd number of spots.

2. There are 13 monkeys at the zoo. If 9 monkeys are swinging from trees, how many monkeys are not swinging from trees?

_____ monkeys are not swinging from trees.

3. $63 + 15 =$

4. $12 - \_\_\_\_ = 7$

5. In the box, draw Base Ten Blocks to show the number 11.

Lesson 62

1. Fill in the blank with <, >, or = to make the number sentence true.

37 _____ 33

2. Circle the even number. 76   89   91

3. $18 - 13 =$

4. $13 + 17 =$

5. $7 + \_\_\_\_ = 14$

Lesson 63

1. Write the numbers in order from least to greatest. 56, 67, 32, 14

   _____, _____, _____, _____

2. 27 – 8 =

3. Write the number ninety-seven. _____

4. Round the number to the nearest tens place. 18 _____

5. Jeremy buys a box of 20 paper clips. He uses 15 paper clips during the school year. How many paper clips does Jeremy have left?

   Jeremy has _____ paper clips left over.

Lesson 64

1. Margaret bought 16 picture frames to give as gifts. Later, she saw a sale on picture frames and bought an additional 14 picture frames. How many picture frames did Margaret buy in all?

   Margaret bought _____ picture frames in all.

2. 34 + 17 =

3. 9 + _____ = 17

4. Write the numbers in order from greatest to least. 17, 77, 21, 38

   _____, _____, _____, _____

5. Look at the Base Ten Blocks. Write the number shown.

   _____

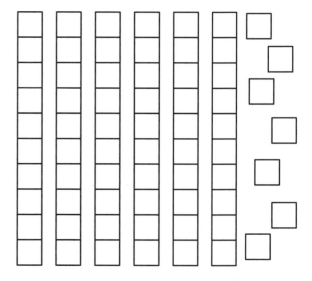

36

Lesson 65

1. Fill in the blank with <, >, or = to make the number sentence true.

    203 _____ 233

2. 5 + 27 =

3. Write the number. 2 hundreds, 5 tens, 6 ones _____

4. 29 + 42 =

5. Write the numbers in order from greatest to least. 14, 41, 33, 46, 45

    _____, _____, _____, _____, _____

Lesson 66

1. LaToya has a vase with 21 roses in it. There are 9 red roses and the rest are white. How many of the roses are white?

    _____ of the roses are white.

2. Write the odd number that is greater than 6, but less than 8.

    _____

3. 200 + 13 =

4. 20 − 12 =

5. Look at the picture. How many frogs are there in all?

    _____

    How many frogs are not touching the lily pad?

    _____

Daily Math Warm-Ups Grade 2

Lesson 67

1. $24 - 6 =$

2. $55 + 16 =$

3. Circle the odd number. 65   32   18

4. Tasha has 16 sweaters. If 9 of the sweaters are wool, how many of the sweaters are not wool?

   _____ of the sweaters are not wool.

5. Write the number eighty.

   _____

Lesson 68

1. $13 - 13 =$

2. Round the number to the nearest tens place.

   77 _____

3. Write the number eighteen.

   _____

4. $18 + 9 =$

5. A large department store sold 25 alarm clocks. By the end of the week, 9 alarm clocks had been returned. How many alarm clocks were not returned?

   _____ of the alarm clocks were not returned.

Lesson 69

1. Circle the even number. 14   91   19

2. A chef cracked 19 eggs. A few minutes later, he cracked an additional 3 eggs. How many eggs did the chef crack in all?

   The chef cracked _____ eggs in all.

3. $15 + 19 =$

4. $22 - 15 =$

5. Look at the picture. How many girls are there in all?

   _____

   How many girls are wearing bows in their hair?

   _____

Lesson 70

1. The tennis club starts its season with 25 tennis balls. During the first week of practice, 16 balls were lost. How many tennis balls are left?

   _____ tennis balls are left.

2. Write the numbers in order from greatest to least. 100, 50, 60, 95

   _____, _____, _____, _____

3. $47 + 37 =$

4. $13 - 5 =$

5. In the box, draw Base Ten Blocks to show 54.

Lesson 71

1. Sasha has 18 magazines about doll collecting and 17 magazines about outdoor games. How many magazines about doll collecting and outdoor games does Sasha have?

   Sasha has _____ magazines about doll collecting and outdoor games.

2. $24 - 15 =$

3. $125 + 10 =$

4. $73 + 14 =$

5. Look at the objects below. Circle all of the cones.

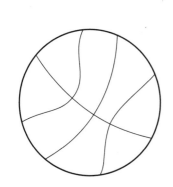   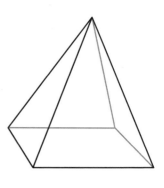

Lesson 72

1. $18 - 9 =$

2. There are 23 colored balls in a bag. If 19 of the balls are brown and the rest are red, how many red balls are in the bag?

   _____ red balls are in the bag.

3. $10 + 224 =$

4. $64 + 19 =$

5. Circle the cylinder.

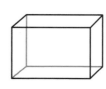  

Lesson 73

1. Mr. Potter has 23 students in his class. If 17 of the students are boys and the rest are girls, how many girls are there in Mr. Potter's class?

    There are _____ girls in Mr. Potter's class.

2. 22 – 7 =

3. Look at the square. Circle the corners.
    A square has _____ corners.

4. 118 + 10 =

5. Look at the objects below. Circle all of the rectangular prisms.

   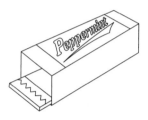

Lesson 74

1. 64 + 35 =

2. How many sides does a triangle have? _____

    How many sides total would 4 triangles have?

    Four triangles have _____ sides total.

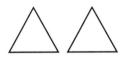

3. 57 – 39 =

4. 319 – 4 =

5. Jamal checked out 18 books from the library in June. He checked out 25 books in July. How many more books did Jamal check out in July than in June?

    Jamal checked out _____ more books in July than in June.

Lesson 75

1. Whitney walked 4 miles on Monday, 4 miles on Tuesday, and 7 miles on Wednesday. How many miles did she walk in all?

    Whitney walked a total of _____ miles.

2. $19 + 48 =$

3. $7 + 19 =$

4. $28 - 19 =$

5. Draw a 😊 in the block 3B.

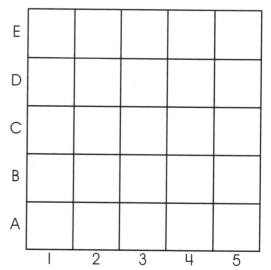

Lesson 76

1. There are 36 computer disks in Lyle's office. If 18 of the disks are already filled with information, how many of the disks are not filled?

    _____ of the disks are not filled.

2. $53 + 24 =$

3. $21 + 19 =$

4. $15 - \underline{\hspace{1cm}} = 9$

5. Circle the 2 figures that are congruent.

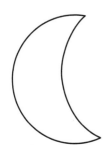    

Lesson 77

1. Draw a  in the block 4E and a ♡ in the block 1C.

2. $27 - 15 =$

3. $200 + 13 =$

4. Circle the cone.

 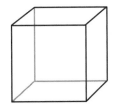

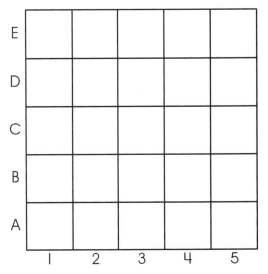

5. Samantha sees 14 butterflies and 12 spiders on a nature walk. How many more butterflies than spiders does Samantha see on her walk?

Samantha sees _____ more butterflies than spiders on her walk.

Lesson 78

1. $17 + 6 =$

2. Crystal and Dante each juggle 11 balls during recess. How many balls do Crystal and Dante juggle in all?

Crystal and Dante juggle _____ balls in all.

3. $22 - 13 =$

4. $25 + 25 =$

5. Color the circle.

Lesson 79

1. A total of 16 students order vegetable sandwiches for lunch. A total of 24 students order turkey sandwiches for lunch. How many students in all order sandwiches for lunch?

   _____ students in all order sandwiches for lunch.

2. 22 – 22 =

3. 69 – 37 =

4. 210 + 10 =

5. Look at the picture. How many faces does the rectangular prism have?

   The rectangular prism has _____ faces.

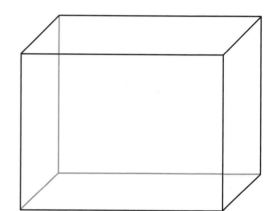

Lesson 80

1. Liza sharpens 11 pencils Monday and 19 pencils Tuesday. How many more pencils does Liza sharpen on Tuesday?

   Liza sharpens _____ more pencils on Tuesday.

2. 17 + 27 =

3. 21 – 17 =

4. 19 + 19 =

5. Circle the shape that has a curved surface.

 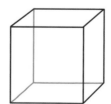 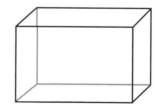

Name _____

Lesson 81

1. Color $\frac{1}{2}$ of the hearts.

2. 500 + 10 =

3. Before lunch, there are 28 cookies in Grandma's cookie jar. After lunch, there are only 19 cookies in Grandma's cookie jar. How many cookies were eaten at lunch?

   _____ cookies were eaten at lunch.

4. 22 + 59 =

5. 450 − 10 =

Lesson 82

1. 250 + 30 =

2. Estimate to the near ___ ball cards. He gives away 12 of his cards ___ yler have left?

   Tyler has about _____ baseball cards left.

3. 12 − 9 =

4. 300 + 60 =

5. Circle the picture that shows $\frac{1}{2}$ of the flowers shaded.

Lesson 83

1. Nikki won 200 prize tickets at the fair on Friday and an additional 35 prize tickets at the fair on Saturday. How many prize tickets did Nikki win in all?

    Nikki earned _____ prize tickets in all.

2. Estimate to the nearest tens place.

    $88 - 26$ is about _____ .

3. Color $\frac{3}{4}$ of the lighthouses.

4. $50 + 50 =$

5. $18 + 17 =$

Lesson 84

1. $32 - 18 =$

2. Jacob writes 27 letters while he is away at camp. He has 19 stamps. How many more stamps does Jacob need to mail all of his letters?

    Jacob needs _____ more stamps to mail all of his letters.

3. $210 + 10 =$

4. $30 - 15 =$

5. Circle the picture that is not symmetrical.

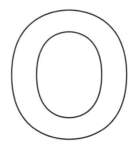

Lesson 85

1. 70 − 55 =

2. 980 + 10 =

3. 130 − 10 =

4. Travon checked out 17 library books. Paul checked out 14 library books. How many library books did Travon and Paul check out altogether?

    Travon and Paul checked out a total of _____ library books.

5. Color $\frac{1}{3}$ of the cats.

Lesson 86

1. Corin blows up 11 green balloons and 19 purple balloons for the school dance. How many total balloons does Corin blow up for the school dance?

    Corin blows up _____ balloons for the school dance.

2. 14 − 9 =

3. 35 + 15 =

4. 70 + 70 =

5. Circle the picture that shows $\frac{1}{4}$ of the leaves shaded.

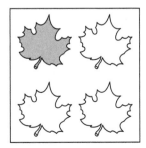  

Lesson 87

1. Estimate to the nearest tens place.

   18 + 18 is about _____ .

2. 80 + 50 =

3. Ms. Owen grades 33 papers on Monday and 19 papers on Tuesday. How many more papers did Ms. Owen grade on Tuesday than on Monday?

   Ms. Owen graded ____ more papers on Tuesday than on Monday.

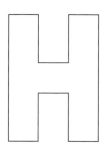

4. 650 − 50 =

5. 75 + 25 =

Lesson 88

1. 260 + 20 =

2. 110 + 4 =

3. 370 − 40 =

4. Eddie washes 26 shirts. He needs to fold 18 shirts. How many shirts does Eddie not need to fold?

   Eddie does not need to fold ____ shirts.

5. Circle the letter that is symmetrical.

 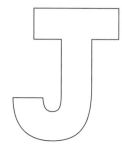

G H J

Lesson 89

1. $119 - 4 =$

2. Mary Ann counts 27 fireflies in her backyard. She catches 11 fireflies in a jar. How many of the fireflies is Mary Ann unable to catch?

    Mary Ann is unable to catch _____ fireflies.

3. $34 - 19 =$

4. $212 + 3 =$

5. Color $\frac{3}{4}$ of the ice cream cones.

Lesson 90

1. Circle the letter that is not symmetrical.

    M R W C

2. $60 + 25 =$

3. $60 - 25 =$

4. Estimate to the nearest tens place. $33 + 47$ is about _____ .

5. Mrs. Dalton buys 27 bottles of water for field day. Ms. Kay buys 36 bottles of water. How many bottles of water do Mrs. Dalton and Ms. Kay buy in all?

    Mrs. Dalton and Ms. Kay buy_____ bottles of water in all.

Lesson 91

1. There are 15 baseball games during the season. If 3 of the games are rained out, how many games are played?

   _____ games are played.

2. 38 + 22 =

3. 13 − 9 =

4. 10 + 138 =

5. What time is shown on the clock? _____

Lesson 92

1. Lenny learned 29 songs in music class. He taught his brother 7 of the new songs on Monday and the rest of the new songs on Wednesday. How many new songs did Lenny teach his brother on Wednesday?

   Lenny taught his brother _____ new songs on Wednesday.

2. 517 + 11 =

3. 220 − 20 =

4. 136 − 6 =

5. Fill in the missing dates to complete the calendar.

November

Sunday	Monday	Tuesday	Wednesday	Thursday	Friday	Saturday
	1	2	3	4	5	
			10			
	22			25		
		30				

Lesson 93

1. What time is shown on the clock?

   _____

2. $300 + 11 =$

3. $15 -$ _____ $= 10$

4. $19 + 300 =$

5. A clown brings 100 lollipops to a party. She gives away all but 20 lollipops. How many lollipops does the clown give away?

   The clown gives away _____ lollipops.

Lesson 94

1. Lacy caught 14 fish one morning. Later the same day, she caught 14 more fish. How many fish did Lacy catch in all?

   Lacy caught _____ fish in all.

2. $210 - 10 =$

3. Write the number. 7 hundreds, 4 tens, 9 ones

   _____

4. $35 + 35 =$

5. What time is shown on the clock?

   _____

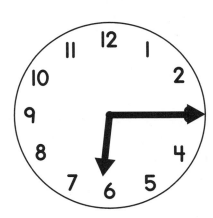

Lesson 95

1. Emma ran 32 minutes on Saturday and 43 minutes on Sunday. How many more minutes did Emma run on Sunday?

   Emma ran _____ more minutes on Sunday.

2. $16 + 25 =$

3. $17 + 36 =$

4. $8 + 48 =$

5. Look at the calendar. What is the date of the first Saturday of the month?

   _____

July

Sunday	Monday	Tuesday	Wednesday	Thursday	Friday	Saturday
1	2	3	4	5	6	7
8	9	10	11	12	13	14
15	16	17	18	19	20	21
22	23	24	25	26	27	28
29	30	31				

Lesson 96

1. Jaime has 47 marbles. If he gives away 28 of his marbles, how many marbles will Jaime have left?

   Jaime will have _____ marbles left.

2. $44 - 9 =$

3. $44 + \_\_\_\_ = 45$

4. $9 + 29 =$

5. Look at the calendar. What day of the week is the ninth of September?

   _____

September

Sunday	Monday	Tuesday	Wednesday	Thursday	Friday	Saturday
			1	2	3	4
5	6	7	8	9	10	11
12	13	14	15	16	17	18
19	20	21	22	23	24	25
26	27	28	29	30		

Lesson 97

1. There are 33 students in Jen's class picture. If 25 of the students are smiling, how many students are not smiling?

   _____ students are not smiling.

2. Estimate to the nearest ten. 56 + 35 is about _____ .

3. $350 - 10 =$

4. $200 + 300 =$

5. What time is shown on the clock?

   _____

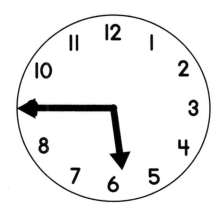

Lesson 98

1. Erin travels 16 miles to get to soccer practice. Tara travels 28 miles to get to soccer practice. How many more miles does Tara travel than Erin?

   Tara travels _____ miles farther than Erin.

2. Round the number to the nearest hundreds place.

   368 _____

3. $222 + 16 =$

4. $890 - 10 =$

5. Look at the clock. What time will it be in 15 minutes?

   _____

Lesson 99

1. Jack has 49 blocks in a bag. If 27 of the blocks are square and the rest are rectangular, how many of the blocks are rectangular?

    _____ of the blocks are rectangular.

2. $19 + 41 =$

3. $100 - 25 =$

4. $338 + 11 =$

5. Look at the clock. What time will it be in 30 minutes?

    _____

Lesson 100

1. Melissa has 33 scarves in her closet. If 19 of the scarves are silk, how many of the scarves are not silk?

    _____ of the scarves are not silk.

2. $500 + 100 =$

3. $10 + 550 =$

4. $17 - 8 =$

5. Look at the calendar. What day of the week is March fifteenth?

    March fifteenth is a

    _____ .

March						
Sunday	Monday	Tuesday	Wednesday	Thursday	Friday	Saturday
					1	2
3	4	5	6	7	8	9
10	11	12	13	14	15	16
17	18	19	20	21	22	23
24 / 31	25	26	27	28	29	30

Lesson 101

1. Jason works on the weekend delivering groceries. On Saturday, he delivers 150 items. On Sunday, he delivers 125 items. How many items does Jason deliver on Saturday and Sunday combined?

   Jason delivers _____ items on Saturday and Sunday combined.

2. $634 + 14 =$

3. $\$3.00 + \$4.00 =$

4. $17 - 9 =$

5. Estimate. Round to the nearest hundreds place.

   $676 + 221$ is about _____ .

Lesson 102

1. Meghan has $0.75. She earns $0.25 more. How much money does Meghan have now?

   Meghan has _____ now.

2. Lindsey has 49 books on her bookshelf. She adds 8 more books after a trip to the bookstore. How many books does Lindsey have now?

   Lindsey has _____ books now.

3. $43 - 17 =$

4. $14 + 16 =$

5. $21 - 19 =$

Lesson 103

1. 39 + 15 =

2. 249 – 18 =

3. 13 – 4 =

4. Cole has $4.00. He earns $2.50 for mowing the lawn. How much money does Cole have now?

    Cole has _____ now.

5. Erika has 178 beads in a container. If 16 beads fall out, how many beads does Erika have left?

    Erika has _____ beads left.

Lesson 104

1. 154 + 13 =

2. 33 – 15 =

3. 500 – 200 =

4. Nell is going to the beach. First, she travels 241 miles by train. Then, she takes a boat for 7 miles. How many miles did Nell travel by train and boat combined?

    Nell traveled _____ miles by train and boat combined.

5. Ella has $0.55. Later, she finds $0.25. How much money does Ella have now?

    Ella has _____ now.

Lesson 105

1. Krystal has $0.92. Her sister gives her $0.08. How much money does Krystal have now?

   Krystal has _____ now.

2. 58 + 14 =

3. Estimate to the nearest hundreds place.

   361 + 325 is about _____ .

4. 550 – 50 =

5. 135 – 14 =

Lesson 106

1. 17 + 17 =

2. 440 + 45 =

3. 61 – 17 =

4. Jocelyn has 200 pieces of candy. She eats 6 pieces of candy. How many pieces of candy does she have left?

   Jocelyn has _____ pieces of candy left.

5. Pedro has $0.78. He spends $0.29 on a baseball card. How much money does Pedro have left?

   Pedro has _____ left.

Lesson 107

1.   28 + 38 =

2.   419 + 4 =

3.   Samuel has a total of $0.33. If he gives away $0.15, how much money will Samuel have left?

     Samuel will have _____ left.

4.   81 − 12 =

5.   Mason records 18 songs on the front of a tape and 17 songs on the back of a tape. How many songs did Mason record on the front and back of the tape altogether?

     Mason recorded _____ songs on the front and back of the tape altogether.

Lesson 108

1. $0.89 − $0.33 =

2.   150 + 50 =

3.   849 − 13 =

4.   512 + 67 =

5.   Anya and Jane grilled 44 hamburgers and 61 hot dogs at their cookout. How many hamburgers and hot dogs did they grill in all?

     Anya and Jane grilled _____ hamburgers and hot dogs in all.

Lesson 109

1. Dylan has $0.38 in his pocket. At lunch, he lends James $0.15. How much money does Dylan have now?

   Dylan has _____ now.

2. $61 + 14 =$

3. $61 - 14 =$

4. $390 + 100 =$

5. Ed spends 40 minutes mowing his front lawn and 15 minutes mowing his back lawn. How many minutes longer does Ed spend mowing his front lawn than his back lawn?

   Ed spends _____ more minutes mowing his front lawn than his back lawn.

Lesson 110

1. Carol planted 132 seeds in her garden. If 100 of the seeds grew into plants, how many seeds did not grow into plants?

   _____ of Carol's seeds did not grow into plants.

2. $511 - 8 =$

3. $918 - 12 =$

4. John started the day with $1.50, but then he lost $0.05. How much money does John have now?

   John has _____ now.

5. $19 + 17 =$

Lesson 111

1. $2.05 − $0.05 =

2. Billy weighs 102 pounds. Harry weighs 9 pounds more than Billy. How much does Harry weigh?

   Harry weighs _____ pounds.

3. 422 + 37 =

4. 44 − 19 =

5. Round to the nearest hundred.

   729 _____

Lesson 112

1. 15 + 205 =

2. 721 − 2 =

3. Mariah has $3.99. After school, she spends $0.50 on a snack. How much money does Mariah have now?

   Mariah has _____ now.

4. 81 + 18 =

5. Virginia stayed at an overnight camp for 14 days. She spent 10 nights in a log cabin and slept in the woods the other nights. How many nights did Virginia sleep in the woods?

   Virginia slept _____ nights in the woods.

Lesson 113

1. $328 - 9 =$

2. $210 + 75 =$

3. $67 - 18 =$

4. Phillip scored 82 points for his basketball team during the regular season. He scored 45 points for his team during the summer season. How many more points did Phillip score during the regular season?

   Phillip scored _____ more points during the regular season.

5. Estimate to the nearest dollar.

   $1.75 + $4.15 is about _____ .

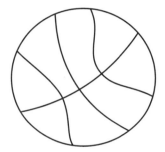

Lesson 114

1. $305 + 37 =$

2. Lori has $3.25. She baby-sits her little sister and earns an additional $4.00. How much money does Lori have now?

   Lori has _____ now.

3. $959 - 100 =$

4. $116 + 9 =$

5. Libby and Cassie are playing a game. Libby has 75 squares. Cassie has 100 squares. How many more squares does Cassie have?

   Cassie has _____ more squares than Libby.

Lesson 115

Name _____

1. $893 - 20 =$

2. $46 + 30 =$

3. $77 + 81 =$

4. Carlos read 28 books in July and 30 books in August. How many more books did Carlos read during August than during July?

   Carlos read _____ more books during August than during July.

5. $\$3.30 + \$2.00 =$

Lesson 116

1. There are 52 dogs walking in Central Park. If 19 of the dogs are barking, how many of the dogs are not barking?

   _____ of the dogs are not barking.

2. $13 - 9 =$

3. $33 - 14 =$

4. $270 + 21 =$

5. $\$6.55 + \$2.20 =$

Lesson 117

1. There are 64 students in the gym. There are 28 boys in the gym. How many girls are in the gym?

    _____ girls are in the gym.

2. Will has $3.50. He loans Todd $1.00. How much money does Will have left?

    Will has _____ left.

3. 650 + 25 =

4. 147 − 16 =

5. 55 + 35 =

Lesson 118

1. 29 + 41 =

2. 130 − 100 =

3. 14 + 88 =

4. $2.75 − $2.00 =

5. Cindy and Mark baked 124 cookies. They sold 100 cookies at the bake sale. How many cookies do Cindy and Mark have left?

    Cindy and Mark have _____ cookies left.

Lesson 119

1. Oscar and Jack traveled 45 miles on Thursday and 58 miles on Friday. How many miles did Oscar and Jack travel in all?

Oscar and Jack traveled _____ miles in all.

2. $171 + 24 =$

3. $990 - 65 =$

4. $\$2.50 + \$2.50 =$

5. $58 + 14 =$

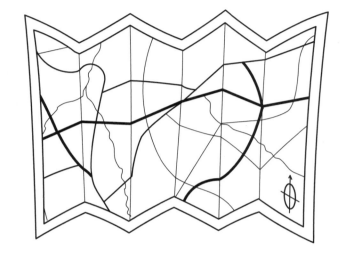

Lesson 120

1. $238 - 15 =$

2. $81 + 19 =$

3. $81 - 19 =$

4. $\$2.29 + \$0.50 =$

5. Of the 74 cars parked in the parking lot, 17 are red. How many of the cars are not red?

_____ of the cars are not red.

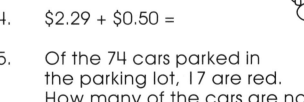

Lesson 121

1. Tim and Connor each went to visit their sisters in different cities. Tim traveled 56 miles to see his sister. Connor traveled 132 miles to see his sister. How many miles did Tim and Connor travel to see their sisters altogether?

   Tim and Connor traveled _____ miles altogether.

2. 33 + 450 =

3. 15 + 19 =

4. 290 – 12 =

5. How many paper clips long is the toothbrush?

   The toothbrush is _____ paper clips long.

Lesson 122

1. On a safari, Mr. Cortez counted 29 lions and 42 giraffes. How many lions and giraffes did Mr. Cortez see in all?

   Mr. Cortez saw _____ lions and giraffes in all.

2. 9 + 8 =

3. 75 + 75 =

4. 314 – 3 =

5. How many cookies long is the cookie tray?

   The cookie tray is _____ cookies in length.

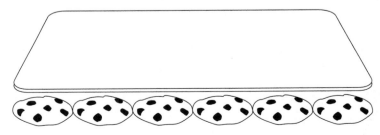

Lesson 123

1. Put the numbers in order from greatest to least.
   72, 71, 76, 56, 54

   _____, _____, _____, _____, _____

2. Tony picked 86 apples one Saturday. If 55 of the apples are red and the rest are green, how many green apples did Tony pick?

   Tony picked _____ green apples.

3. 62 + 58 =

4. 626 – 14 =

5. Look at the pictures. Circle the heaviest object.

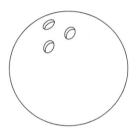

Lesson 124

1. Wilson spent 45 hours working one week and 52 hours working the next week. How many hours did Wilson work during the two weeks combined?

   Wilson spent _____ hours working during the two weeks combined.

2. Put the numbers in order from least to greatest. 117, 71, 88, 35, 46

   _____, _____, _____, _____, _____

3. 22 + 88 =

4. 97 + 21 =

5. Look at the picture. How many inches long is the picture frame?

   The picture frame is _____ inches long.

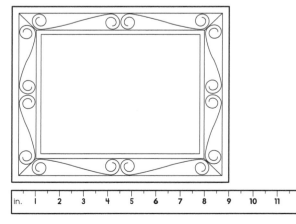

Name _____

Lesson 125

1. The teacher set up 79 chairs in the school cafeteria. Later, she set up an additional 21 chairs. How many chairs did the teacher set up in all?

   The teacher set up _____ chairs.

2. Draw an X on each even number.

   17   33   134   48   190

3. 62 + 15 =

4. 62 − 15 =

5. Look at the picture. How many centimeters long is the bandage?

   The bandage is _____ centimeters long.

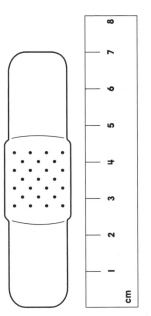

Lesson 126

1. Put the numbers in order from least to greatest. 216, 129, 312, 99, 493

   _____, _____, _____, _____, _____

2. Room 2-B recycles 100 cans during May and 75 cans during June. How many more cans does Room 2-B recycle during May?

   Room 2-B recycles _____ more cans during May.

3. 34 − 28 =

4. 272 + 13 =

5. Look at the picture. How many inches long is the watch?

   The watch is _____ inches long.

Lesson 127

1. Circle the unit that would be most likely used to measure the length of a football field.

   inch   foot   yard   mile

2. Dominic received 89 letters in March and 56 letters in April. How many letters did Dominic receive in March and April total?

   Dominic received _____ letters in March and April total.

3. $49 - 17 =$

4. $45 + 50 =$

5. For each of the following numbers, circle the number in the tens place.

   74   456   31   190   123

Lesson 128

1. If 68 children signed up to play lacrosse and 74 children signed up to play soccer, how many more children signed up to play soccer?

   _____ more children signed up to play soccer.

2. $444 - 13 =$

3. Circle the odd number.

   318   151   220   100

4. $56 + 111 =$

5. Look at the picture. How many erasers long is the chalkboard?

   The chalkboard is _____ erasers long.

Lesson 129

1. Henry found 38 shells on the first day of vacation. On the second day, he found 45 more shells. On the third day, he found 38 more shells. How many shells did Henry find on the first and third days of vacation combined?

   Henry found _____ shells during the first and third days of vacation.

2. $19 - 7 =$

3. $44 + 15 =$

4. Look at the picture. How many inches long is the hammer?

   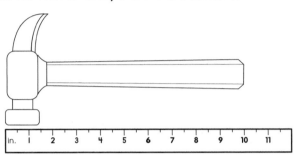

   The hammer is _____ inches long.

5. Put the numbers in order from greatest to least. 101, 115, 111, 133, 122

   _____, _____, _____, _____, _____

Lesson 130

1. Mrs. Carter ordered 17 watermelons for the school picnic. If 11 of the watermelons were delivered on time and the rest of the watermelons were delivered late, how many watermelons were delivered late?

   _____ watermelons were delivered late.

2. Circle the even number.
   756   429   831   211

3. $231 - 13 =$

4. $164 + 9 =$

5. How many pounds does the baby weigh?

   The baby weighs _____ pounds.

Lesson 131

1. There are 39 footballs and 45 basketballs in the gym. How many footballs and basketballs are there in all?

   There are _____ footballs and basketballs in all.

2. Look at the picture graph. How many more cookies were baked for the spring bake sale than the fall bake sale?

   _____ more cookies were baked for the spring bake sale than the fall bake sale.

3. $9 + \_\_\_\_ = 18$

4. $29 + 29 =$

5. $32 - 18 =$

Cookies Baked for the Bake Sale

= 10 cookies

Fall
Spring
Summer

Lesse...

1. A group ... camping trip. If 7 kids forgot to pack their sleeping b... ...s remembered to pack their sleeping bags?

   _____ kids reme... ...ered to pack their sleeping bags.

2. $12 - \_\_\_\_ = 4$

3. $71 - 18 =$

4. $631 - 15 =$

5. Look at the bar graph. How many cans of juice were sold on Saturday and Sunday?

   _____ cans of juice were sold on Saturday and Sunday.

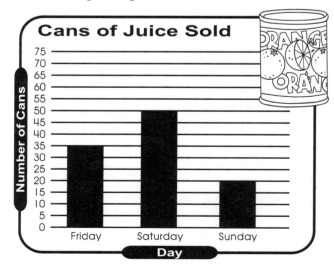

Cans of Juice Sold

Number of Cans

75
70
65
60
55
50
45
40
35
30
25
20
15
10
5
0

Friday   Saturday   Sunday
Day

Lesson 133

Name _____

1. 333 + 444 =

2. 200 + 40 =

3. Look at the table. Based on the information, which day was the warmest?

    _____ was the warmest day.

Weather in My City	
Day	**Temperature**
Monday	67° F
Tuesday	65° F
Wednesday	74° F
Thursday	81° F
Friday	68° F

4. 90 – 61 =

5. Paul has 2 boxes of old records in his garage. He has 57 records in one box and 61 records in another box. How many records does Paul have in both boxes combined?

    Paul has a total of _____ records in both boxes combined.

Lesson 134

1. Look at the tally chart. How many pennies did the girls spend altogether?

    The girls spent _____ pennies altogether.

Number of Pennies Spent		
Rebecca	Jana	Suki
⊞⊞	⊞⊞	⊞⊞
⊞⊞	⊞⊞	⊞⊞
|	||||	⊞⊞ ||

2. 616 – 11 =

3. 102 + 80 =

4. 41 – 17 =

5. Pamela collects magazines. She has 88 magazines. Her sister gives her 18 more magazines. How many magazines does Pamela have now?

    Pamela has _____ magazines now.

Lesson 135

1. The baker frosted 120 out of 251 cupcakes with vanilla icing. He frosted the remaining cupcakes with chocolate icing. How many cupcakes did the baker frost with chocolate icing?

   The baker frosted _____ cupcakes with chocolate icing.

2. Look at the picture graph. How many children voted for their favorite shape?

   _____ children voted for their favorite shape.

3. $541 - 230 =$

4. $12 + 8 =$

5. $410 + 180 =$

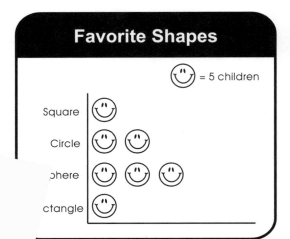

Lesson 136

1. Look at the table. Based on the information, which grade has the fewest girls?

   Grade _____ has the fewest girls.

2. $105 + 260 =$

3. $960 - 740 =$

4. $233 + 214 =$

5. A toy store has 82 red wagons for sale. It sells 59 red wagons on Saturday. How many red wagons are left?

   _____ red wagons are left.

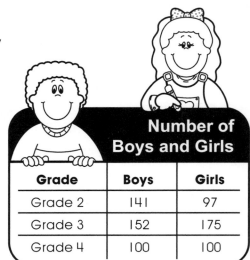

Lesson 137

1. Look at the bar graph. How many trains passed through the station at 7 A.M. and 9 P.M. combined?

    _____ trains passed through the station at 7 A.M. and 9 P.M. combined.

2. $22 - 10 =$

3. $14 + 19 =$

4. $21 + 3 =$

5. Jenny is reading a book that is 98 pages long. She has read 47 pages so far. How many pages does Jenny have left to read?

    Jenny has _____ pages left to read.

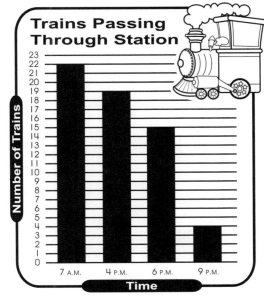

Trains Passing Through Station

Number of Trains / Time (7 A.M., 4 P.M., 6 P.M., 9 P.M.)

Lesson 138

1. There are 153 kids enrolled in summer camp. If 70 of the kids are boys and the rest are girls, how many girls are enrolled in summer camp?

    _____ girls are enrolled in summer camp.

2. Look at the tally chart. How many more games did Quinn win than Rory?

    Quinn won _____ more games than Rory.

3. $140 - 121 =$

4. $16 + 16 =$

5. $16 - 16 =$

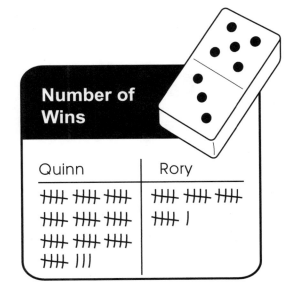

Number of Wins

Quinn	Rory
卌 卌 卌 卌 卌 卌 卌 卌 卌 卌 |||	卌 卌 卌 卌	

Lesson 139

1. Look at the picture graph. How many more cards does Group 2 have than Group 3?

   Group 2 has _____ more cards than Group 3.

2. $300 + 64 =$

3. $95 - 30 =$

4. $50 + 125 =$

5. Oscar and Bebe invited 137 people to their wedding. If 9 people were not able to attend, how many people were able to attend their wedding?

   _____ people were able to attend the wedding.

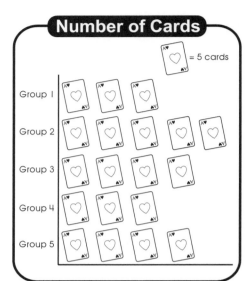

Lesson 140

1. Look at the bar graph. How many more students walk or ride the bus to school than ride in a car?

   _____ more students walk or ride the bus than ride in a car.

2. $191 + 6 =$

3. $375 - 15 =$

4. $500 + 100 =$

5. A total of 152 students attended the school dance. If 49 students went home before 8 P.M., how many students went home after 8 P.M.?

   _____ students went home after 8 P.M.

Lesson 141

1. If 274 people attended the baseball game and 56 people won free T-shirts, how many people at the game did not win T-shirts?

    _____ people at the game did not win T-shirts.

2. Estimate to the nearest hundred. 359 + 662 is about _____ .

3. 314 + 18 =

4. 142 + 89 =

5. Draw the missing bananas to complete the pattern.

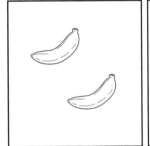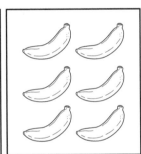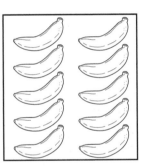

Lesson 142

1. 700 – 200 =

2. 333 – 111 =

3. 19 + 5 =

4. There are 24 students in Room 2-L. Out of those 24, 15 of the students are wearing jeans. How many of the students are not wearing jeans?

    _____ of the students are not wearing jeans.

5. Write the missing number to complete the pattern.

    900, 700, 500, _____, 100

Lesson 143

1. A total of 159 children entered a coloring contest. If 15 children won a ribbon, how many children did not win a ribbon?

   _____ children did not win a ribbon.

2. $214 - 5 =$

3. Estimate to the nearest ten.

   $117 + 113$ is about _____ .

4. $111 + 145 =$

5. Draw an X on all the odd numbers.

54 65 43 21 19 71 49 50

Lesson 144

1. Fill in the blank with >,<, or = to make the number sentence true.

   278 _____ 317

2. $19 + 84 =$

3. Draw the missing shapes to complete the pattern.

   ◯ ▢ ▢ △ ◯ ▢ ▢ △ ◯ ▢ ___ ___

4. $14 + 26 =$

5. Ben has 120 flash cards. If 11 flash cards show subtraction facts and the rest of the flash cards show addition facts, how many flash cards show addition facts?

   _____ flash cards show addition facts.

Lesson 145

1. Estimate to the nearest ten.

    545 + 129 is about _____ .

2. Allison bakes 14 loaves of bread. She gives away 8 loaves of bread. How many loaves of bread does Allison have left?

    Allison has _____ loaves of bread left.

3. 55 − 5 =

4. 13 − 7 =

5. Fill in the blank with >,<, or = to make the number sentence true.

    55 _____ 55

Lesson 146

1. Estimate to the nearest ten.

    56 + 33 is about _____ .

2. 14 − 7 =

3. 683 + 12 =

4. Ollie has 98 coins in his bank. He gives away 17 coins. How many coins does he have left?

    Ollie has _____ coins left.

5. Write the missing numbers to complete the pattern.

    17, 15, 13, 11, _____, 7, _____

Lesson 147

1. $16 - 3 =$

2.   Estimate to the nearest hundred.

      $444 + 313$ is about _____ .

3. $78 + 59 =$

4.   Write the missing numbers to complete the pattern.

      350, 300, 250, _____ , 150, _____

5.   Sabena scored 12 points during her Monday night basketball game. On Tuesday night, she scored an additional 22 points. How many points did Sabena score in all?

      Sabena scored _____ points in all.

Lesson 148

1.   Brianna has 81 green beads, 71 red beads, and 77 purple beads on her necklace. How many purple and green beads are on Brianna's necklace?

      _____ purple and green beads are on Brianna's necklace.

2. $15 - 9 =$

3. $333 - 4 =$

4. $215 + 251 =$

5.   Draw the missing rectangles to complete the pattern.

Lesson 149

1. Estimate to the nearest hundred.

    433 + 226 is about _____ .

2. 16 + 9 =

3. 16 − 9 =

4. Write the missing letter to complete the pattern.

    F, G, H, J, K, L, N, _____ , P, R

5. There are 55 spices on a shelf. A chef uses 17 spices in a secret recipe. How many spices does the chef not use?

    The chef does not use _____ spices.

Lesson 150

1. There are 15 kids waiting in line. Andre is 8th in line. How many kids are behind Andre in line?

    _____ kids are behind Andre in line.

2. 27 − 18 =

3. 600 − 200 =

4. 88 + 88 =

5. Draw the missing object to complete the pattern.

 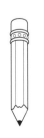 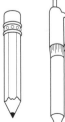  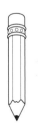 

_____

Lesson 151

1. There are 19 trees in Lynn's front yard and 27 trees in her backyard. How many trees total are there in Lynn's front yard and backyard?

    There are _____ trees in Lynn's front yard and backyard.

2. Look at the Base Ten Blocks. Write the number shown.

    _____

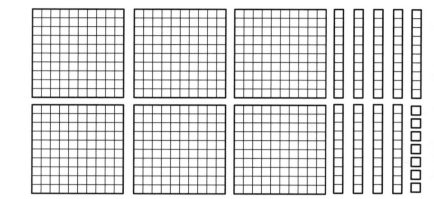

3. $18 + 18 =$

4. $727 - 9 =$

5. Write the number two hundred seven.

    _____

Lesson 152

1. A total of 38 people are waiting for a bus to take them to Atlanta. Later, 5 more people arrive to wait for the bus. How many people are waiting for the bus now?

    _____ people are waiting for the bus now.

2. $337 - 330 =$

3. Write the number one hundred eighteen.

    _____

4. $255 + 130 =$

5. In the box, draw Base Ten Blocks to show the number 210.

Lesson 153

1. $71 - 6 =$

2. There are 123 fish swimming in a lake. If 13 of the fish are caught, how many fish are left in the lake?

    _____ fish are left in the lake.

3. $259 + 8 =$

4. Write the number seven hundred two. _____

5. Circle the greatest number.   156   173   123

Lesson 154

1. Look at the Base Ten Blocks. Write the number shown.

    _____

2. $81 - 18 =$

3. $29 + 14 =$

4. $51 - 17 =$

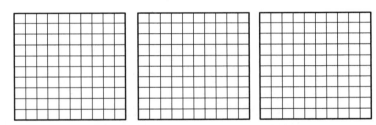
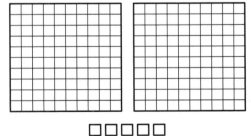

5. Use the following clues to write a 3-digit number.

    The digit in the tens place is 3.
    The digit in the hundreds place is greater than 5 and less than 7.
    The only remaining digit is a 0. What is the number?

    The number is _____ .

Lesson 155

1. What number comes right after 576?

    _____

2. Circle the even number that is least.   16   1   32   12   19

3. $221 + 447 =$

4. $84 - 41 =$

5. $98 + 56 =$

Lesson 156

1. $91 - 50 =$

2. $550 + 24 =$

3. Ellie eats 19 strawberries and Emma eats 27 strawberries. How many more strawberries does Emma eat than Ellie?

    Emma eats _____ more strawberries than Ellie.

4. $75 + 15 =$

5. In the box, draw Base Ten Blocks to show the number 703.

Lesson 157

1. $61 - 12 =$

2. $14 - 8 =$

3. $717 - 111 =$

4.   Write the number four hundred thirteen.

   _____

5.   There are 16 students in Ms. Searcy's class and 22 students in Mr. Spencer's class. How many more students are in Mr. Spencer's class than Ms. Searcy's class?

   There are _____ more students in Mr. Spencer's class than in Ms. Searcy's.

Lesson 158

1. $18 - 4 =$

2. $29 + 29 =$

3.   It rains 9 days in May, 6 days in June, and 4 days in July. How many days does it rain during May and July?

   It rains _____ days during May and July.

4.   Write the number three hundred sixty.

   _____

5.   Use the following clues to write a 3-digit number.

   The three digits in this number are 6, 5, and 2.
   The digit in the ones place is greater than 1, but less than 4.
   The largest digit belongs in the tens place. What is the number?

   The number is _____ .

Name _____

Lesson 159

1. 162 + 17 =

2. 700 – 300 =

3. What is the value of the 5 in the number 564?

    _____

4. Write the number one hundred one.

    _____

5. A total of 74 people order vegetable soup at the deli. A total of 51 people order chili at the deli. How many more people order vegetable soup than chili?

    _____ more people order vegetable soup than chili.

Lesson 160

1. 28 + 6 =

2. Jackie jumps rope for 31 minutes Saturday and 27 minutes Sunday. How many more minutes does Jackie jump rope on Saturday than on Sunday?

    Jackie jumps rope _____ more minutes on Saturday than on Sunday.

3. 200 + 650 =

4. 9 + 14 =

5. Look at the Base Ten Blocks. Write the number shown.

    _____

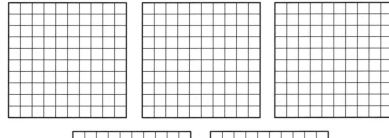

Lesson 161

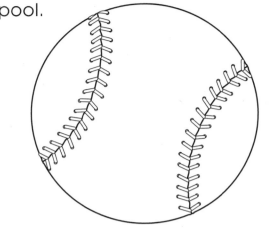

1. Jesse invited 18 friends over to swim in his pool. A group of 13 boys jumped in the pool as soon as they arrived. The remaining boys played a game of baseball. How many boys played baseball?

   _____ boys played baseball.

2. $72 + 16 =$

3. $106 + 211 =$

4. $34 - 29 =$

5. There are 115 first graders and 254 second graders at Kenworth Elementary School. How many first and second graders in all?

   There are _____ first and second graders in all.

Lesson 162

1. Patrick scored 14 goals in September, 8 goals in October, and 12 goals in November. How many more goals did Patrick score in September than October?

   Patrick scored _____ more goals in September than in October.

2. $345 - 111 =$

3. $222 + 333 =$

4. $18 + 47 =$

5. $121 + 450 =$

Lesson 163

1.   150 + 234 =

2.   275 − 50 =

3.   26 + 19 =

4.   Cameron sees 89 ducks in a pond. He sees 19 ducks fly away. How many ducks are left?

      _____ ducks are left.

5.   541 + 234 =

Lesson 164

1.   If 115 people live on Mulberry Street and 15 of the people are children, how many of the people are not children?

      _____ of the people on Mulberry Street are not children.

2.   118 + 111 =

3.   778 − 216 =

4.   90 + 90 =

5.   789 − 645 =

Lesson 165

1. 302 + 407 =

2. 29 + 55 =

3. There are 199 boats on the lake. Of those, 103 boats are sailboats. How many of the boats are not sailboats?

    _____ of the boats are not sailboats.

4. 611 + 310 =

5. 45 + 45 =

Lesson 166

1. 129 + 324 =

2. 51 + 36 =

3. 270 – 65 =

4. 543 + 239 =

5. The Swanson family drove to the beach for summer vacation. They drove 114 miles on Thursday and 108 miles on Friday. How many miles did they drive total?

    They drove a total of _____ miles.

Lesson 167

1.   119 + 235 =

2.   106 + 112 =

3.   800 + 100 =

4.   Katie mailed 117 letters. Because they had the wrong zip code on them, 51 letters were returned. How many letters were not returned?

   _____ letters were not returned.

5.   800 – 110 =

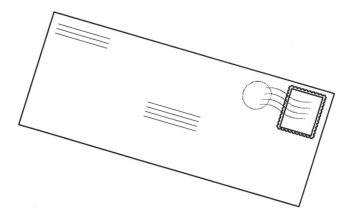

Lesson 168

1.   181 + 14 =

2.   Jackson sent 3 notes to his friends on Monday and 15 notes to his friends on Wednesday. How many more notes did Jackson send on Wednesday?

   Jackson sent _____ more notes on Wednesday.

3.   790 – 560 =

4.   801 + 202 =

5.   207 + 207 =

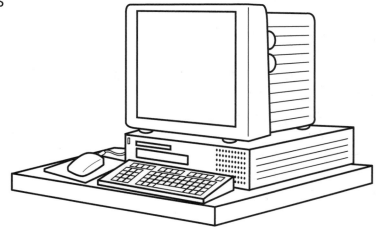

88

Lesson 169

1. $172 + 18 =$

2. $700 + 300 =$

3. $600 - 555 =$

4. $294 - 71 =$

5.   The science teacher teaches 314 students on Monday and 156 students on Tuesday. How many students does the science teacher teach on Monday and Tuesday?

The science teacher teaches _____ students on Monday and Tuesday.

Lesson 170

1. $708 - 449 =$

2. $55 - 38 =$

3. $114 + 131 =$

4.   The snack bar has 350 cups at the beginning of the afternoon. By the end of the afternoon, it only has 171 cups left. How many cups did the snack bar use?

The snack bar used _____ cups.

5. $333 + 167 =$

Lesson 171

1. 809 − 299 =

2. Estimate to the nearest tens place.

    264 + 533 is about _____ .

3. 115 + 201 =

4. 32 − 19 =

5. Hannah has 3 containers of tennis balls. Each container holds 3 tennis balls. How many tennis balls does Hannah have in all?

    Hannah has a total of _____ tennis balls.

Lesson 172

1. 233 + 459 =

2. 150 + 117 =

3. 87 − 54 =

4. 900 − 200 =

5. There are 5 airplanes getting ready for takeoff. Each airplane has 2 wings. How many wings do the airplanes have altogether?

    The airplanes have _____ wings altogether.

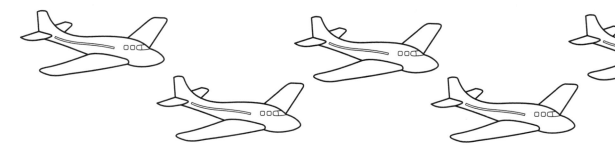

Lesson 173

1. In the box, draw circles to show the number sentence 2 x 3 = .

2. 19 + 113 =

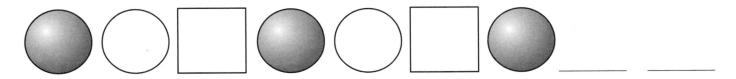

3. Courtney made 81 cookies for a bake sale. She sold all but 9 of the cookies. How many cookies did Courtney sell?

   Courtney sold _____ cookies.

4. 91 – 87 =

5. Draw the missing shapes to complete the pattern.

Lesson 174

1. Write the missing numbers to complete the pattern.

   17, 21, _____, _____, 33

2. If 3 bicycles each have 2 wheels, how many wheels do all 3 bicycles have?

   The bicycles have a total of _____ wheels.

3. 59 + 8 =

4. 59 – 8 =

5. Mrs. Benson ordered 264 cartons of chocolate milk and 351 cartons of plain milk. How many cartons did Mrs. Benson order in all?

   Mrs. Benson ordered a total of _____ cartons in all.

Lesson 175

Name _____

1. $186 + 239 =$

2. $101 + 54 =$

3. There are 2 magazines on a table. Each magazine has 10 pages. How many pages are in both magazines total?

   There are _____ pages in both magazines total.

4. $81 + 109 =$

5. Draw the missing shapes to complete the pattern.

Lesson 176

1. Write the missing letters to complete the pattern.
   A, D, G, _____, M, _____, S

2. Matt has 62 practice balls in his bag. His baby cousin takes out 7 balls. How many practice balls does Matt have left in his bag?

   Matt has _____ practice balls left in his bag.

3. $76 + 76 =$

4. $250 - 125 =$

5. There are 2 monkeys swinging in a tree. Each monkey is holding 3 bananas. How many bananas are the 2 monkeys holding altogether?

   The 2 monkeys are holding a total of _____ bananas.

Lesson 177

1. 89 + 6 =

2. Fill in the blank with >,<, or = to make the number sentence true.
    113 _____ 131

3. 162 + 715 =

4. 5 + _____ = 13

5. A group of 4 families have their pictures taken. There are 5 people in each family. How many people are there in the 4 families combined?

    There are _____ people in the 4 families combined.

Lesson 178

1. Emily and Rebecca are placing all of their teddy bears on a bookshelf in their room. The bookshelf has 4 shelves. They place 4 teddy bears on each shelf. How many teddy bears are on all 4 shelves total?

    There are _____ teddy bears on all 4 shelves total.

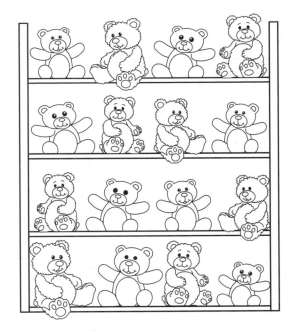

2. 22 + 110 =

3. 34 – 17 =

4. 95 + 210 =

5. A group of 100 students were planning to go on a field trip. If 7 of the students got sick and could not go, how many students were able to go on the field trip?

    _____ students were able to go on the field trip.

Lesson 179

1. Kimberly pours glasses of lemonade for 4 children. Each child drinks 2 glasses of lemonade. How many glasses of lemonade does Kimberly pour in all?

   Kimberly pours _____ glasses of lemonade in all.

2. $49 - 7 =$

3. $61 + 73 =$

4. $44 + 112 =$

5. Tamika picks up 102 rocks when she is at the beach. She gives her brother 49 of the rocks she collects. How many rocks does Tamika have left?

   Tamika has _____ rocks left.

Lesson 180

1. There are 3 stacks of books on a table. There are 5 books in each stack. How many books are there in all?

   There are _____ books in all.

2. $162 + 31 =$

3. $215 + 367 =$

4. $228 - 119 =$

5. Derrik made 37 calls in the morning and 54 calls in the afternoon. How many more calls did Derrik make in the afternoon?

   Derrik made _____ more calls in the afternoon.

Answer Key: Lessons 1–23

Lesson 1
1. 16
2. 7
3. 3
4. 5
5. 6 − 2 = 4; 4

Lesson 2
1. 7
2. 9
3. 1
4. 8
5. 17 − 7 = 10

Lesson 3
1. 19
2. 11
3. 5
4. 5 − 3 = 2; 2
5. 16

Lesson 4
1. 6 − 2 = 4; 4
2. 6; 8; 12
3. 9
4. 10
5. 20

Lesson 5
1. 14
2. 2 + 3 = 5; 5
3. 8
4. 2
5. ▭▭▭▭▭▭
    ▭▭▭▭▭▭

Lesson 6
1. 10
2. 12
3. 2
4. 18
5. 7 + 6 = 13; 13

Lesson 7
1. 16
2. 9
3. 3
4. 3
5. 4, 6, 11, 12, 16

Lesson 8
1. 9
2. 6 + 4 = 10; 10
3. 1
4. 17
5. 16

Lesson 9
1. 1 circled; 8 crossed out
2. 5 − 3 = 2; 2
3. 10
4. 1
5. 2, 7, 10, 14, 15

Lesson 10
1. 9 − 7 = 2; 2
2. 15
3. 11
4. 4
5. 17, 13, 9, 5, 3

Lesson 11
1. 11
2. 12
3. 4
4. 18
5. 13 − 3 = 10

Lesson 12
1. circle drawn
2. 12 + 5 = 17; 17
3. 16
4. 16; 22
5. 6

Lesson 13
1. 12 − 9 = 3; 3
2. 18
3. 2
4. 15
5. 4 − 2 = 2 objects drawn

Lesson 14
1. 11 − 2 = 9; 9
2. 19
3. 22; 26
4. 16
5. 14

Lesson 15
1. 5
2. 10 − 4 = 6 objects drawn
3. 0
4. 8
5. 20

Lesson 16
1. 6
2. 10
3. 18
4. 15
5. R; T

Lesson 17
1. 18
2. 4 + 6 = 10 objects drawn
3. 20
4. 6
5. 18

Lesson 18
1. 16
2. 6
3. 2
4. 4
5. 9 + 3 = 12

Lesson 19
1. 25; 30
2. 3
3. 7 + 7 = 14
4. 15
5. 16

Lesson 20
1. 20
2. 8
3. 16
4. 7 − 3 = 4; 4
5. heart drawn

Lesson 21
1. 6
2. 10
3. 10
4. 6
5. 5 + 6 = 11; 11

Lesson 22
1. 8
2. 18
3. 12
4. 12
5. 11

Lesson 23
1. 3
2. 12
3. 13
4. 5
5. 10

Answer Key: Lessons 24–46

Lesson 24
1. 2
2. 40; 45
3. 20
4. 3
5. 11

Lesson 25
1. 9
2. 26
3. 0
4. 13
5. 27

Lesson 26
1. Hockey
2. 1
3. 17
4. 6
5. 30

Lesson 27
1. 22
2. 29
3. 11
4. 11
5. 2

Lesson 28
1. 3
2. 28
3. 38
4. 20
5. 5

Lesson 29
1. 7
2. 30; 40
3. 39
4. 9
5. A circled

Lesson 30
1. 6
2. 5
3. 11
4. 30
5. 13

Lesson 31
1. 11
2. 2 circled
3. 7
4. 27
5. 16

Lesson 32
1. 7 circled
2. 4
3. 24
4. 16
5. 15

Lesson 33
1. 13
2. 11
3. 25
4. 27
5. 20

Lesson 34
1. 13
2. 70; 100
3. 2
4. 22
5. 2

Lesson 35
1. 22 circled
2. 30
3. 2
4. 10
5. 30

Lesson 36
1. 21
2. 23
3. 11
4. 28
5. 87

Lesson 37
1. 6
2. 22
3. 48
4. 12
5. 30

Lesson 38
1. 6
2. 90; 95
3. 39
4. 10
5. 64

Lesson 39
1. 97
2. 31
3. 19 circled
4. 88
5. 12

Lesson 40
1. 11
2. 20
3. Yellow
4. 53
5. 100

Lesson 41
1. 11
2. 19
3. 2
4. 12
5. 9 rocks drawn

Lesson 42
1. 68
2. 25; 20
3. 14
4. 2
5. 20, 30, 60, 70, 80, 90

Lesson 43
1. 28
2. 10
3. 5
4. 19 beans drawn
5. 2

Lesson 44
1. 20; 30
2. 4
3. 45
4. 23
5. 25

Lesson 45
1. 30
2. 70
3. 3
4. 18
5. 6 buttons drawn

Lesson 46
1. 18
2. 7
3. 11
4. 3
5. N, O

Answer Key: Lessons 47–68

Lesson 47
1. 29
2. D circled
3. 38
4. 94
5. 62

Lesson 48
1. cow; pig
2. 13
3. 48
4. 77
5. 10

Lesson 49
1. 14
2. 30
3. 23
4. 2
5. 13

Lesson 50
1. 37
2. 31
3. 3
4. 56
5. J; P

Lesson 51
1. 34
2. 10 centimeters circled
3. 32
4. 6
5. D circled

Lesson 52
1. 80
2. 10
3. 7
4. 31
5. >

Lesson 53
1. 30
2. C circled
3. 35
4. 7
5. 3

Lesson 54
1. 31
2. 60
3. 58
4. 20
5. B circled

Lesson 55
1. 2
2. 40
3. =
4. 23
5. 56

Lesson 56
1. 80
2. 22
3. 3
4. 8
5. 22

Lesson 57
1. 33
2. $14 - 8 = 6$
3. 31
4. 60
5. 10

Lesson 58
1. 5
2. 32
3. 9
4. 30
5. $13 - 4 = 9$

Lesson 59
1. 31
2. 34
3. 23
4. 3
5. $3 + 15 = 18$

Lesson 60
1. 30
2. 9
3. 5
4. 90
5. 14

Lesson 61
1. middle dog circled
2. 4
3. 78
4. 5
5.

Lesson 62
1. >
2. 76 circled
3. 5
4. 30
5. 7

Lesson 63
1. 14, 32, 56, 67
2. 19
3. 97
4. 20
5. 5

Lesson 64
1. 30
2. 51
3. 8
4. 77, 38, 21, 17
5. 67

Lesson 65
1. <
2. 32
3. 256
4. 71
5. 46, 45, 41, 33, 14

Lesson 66
1. 12
2. 7
3. 213
4. 8
5. 3; 2

Lesson 67
1. 18
2. 71
3. 65 circled
4. 7
5. 80

Lesson 68
1. 0
2. 80
3. 18
4. 27
5. 16

Answer Key: Lessons 69–88

Lesson 69
1. 14 circled
2. 22
3. 34
4. 7
5. 4; 3

Lesson 70
1. 9
2. 100, 95, 60, 50
3. 84
4. 8
5.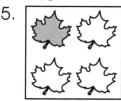

Lesson 71
1. 35
2. 9
3. 135
4. 87
5. ice cream cone, party hat circled

Lesson 72
1. 9
2. 4
3. 234
4. 83
5. cylinder circled

Lesson 73
1. 6
2. 15
3. 4 corners circled; 4
4. 128
5. tissue box, gum package circled

Lesson 74
1. 99
2. 3; 12
3. 18
4. 315
5. 7

Lesson 75
1. 15
2. 67
3. 26
4. 9
5.

Lesson 76
1. 18
2. 77
3. 40
4. 6
5. first and last crescents circled

Lesson 77
1.

2. 12
3. 213
4. cone circled
5. 2

Lesson 78
1. 23
2. 22
3. 9
4. 50
5. circle colored

Lesson 79
1. 40
2. 0
3. 32
4. 220
5. 6

Lesson 80
1. 8
2. 44
3. 4
4. 38
5. cone circled

Lesson 81
1.
2. 510
3. 9
4. 81
5. 440

Lesson 82
1. 280
2. 20
3. 3
4. 360
5.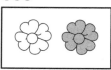

Lesson 83
1. 235
2. 60
3.
4. 100
5. 35

Lesson 84
1. 14
2. 8
3. 220
4. 15
5. girl circled

Lesson 85
1. 15
2. 990
3. 120
4. 31
5. 1 cat colored

Lesson 86
1. 30
2. 5
3. 50
4. 140
5.

Lesson 87
1. 40
2. 130
3. 14
4. 600
5. 100

Lesson 88
1. 280
2. 114
3. 330
4. 8
5. H circled

Answer Key: Lessons 89–111

Lesson 89
1. 115
2. 16
3. 15
4. 215
5. 3 ice cream cones colored

Lesson 90
1. R circled
2. 85
3. 35
4. 80
5. 63

Lesson 91
1. 12
2. 60
3. 4
4. 148
5. 2:00

Lesson 92
1. 22
2. 528
3. 200
4. 130
5.

November						
Sunday	Monday	Tuesday	Wednesday	Thursday	Friday	Saturday
	1	2	3	4	5	6
7	8	9	10	11	12	13
14	15	16	17	18	19	20
21	22	23	24	25	26	27
28	29	30				

Lesson 93
1. 4:30
2. 311
3. 5
4. 319
5. 80

Lesson 94
1. 28
2. 200
3. 749
4. 70
5. 6:15

Lesson 95
1. 11
2. 41
3. 53
4. 56
5. July 7

Lesson 96
1. 19
2. 35
3. 1
4. 38
5. Thursday

Lesson 97
1. 8
2. 90
3. 340
4. 500
5. 5:45

Lesson 98
1. 12
2. 400
3. 238
4. 880
5. 1:45

Lesson 99
1. 22
2. 60
3. 75
4. 349
5. 6:30

Lesson 100
1. 14
2. 600
3. 560
4. 9
5. Friday

Lesson 101
1. 275
2. 648
3. $7.00
4. 8
5. 900

Lesson 102
1. $1.00
2. 57
3. 26
4. 30
5. 2

Lesson 103
1. 54
2. 231
3. 9
4. $6.50
5. 162

Lesson 104
1. 167
2. 18
3. 300
4. 248
5. $0.80

Lesson 105
1. $1.00
2. 72
3. 700
4. 500
5. 121

Lesson 106
1. 34
2. 485
3. 44
4. 194
5. $0.49

Lesson 107
1. 66
2. 423
3. $0.18
4. 69
5. 35

Lesson 108
1. $0.56
2. 200
3. 836
4. 579
5. 105

Lesson 109
1. $0.23
2. 75
3. 47
4. 490
5. 25

Lesson 110
1. 32
2. 503
3. 906
4. $1.45
5. 36

Lesson 111
1. $2.00
2. 111
3. 459
4. 25
5. 700

Answer Key: Lessons 112–133

Lesson 112
1. 220
2. 719
3. $3.49
4. 99
5. 4

Lesson 113
1. 319
2. 285
3. 49
4. 37
5. $6.00

Lesson 114
1. 342
2. $7.25
3. 859
4. 125
5. 25

Lesson 115
1. 873
2. 76
3. 158
4. 2
5. $5.30

Lesson 116
1. 33
2. 4
3. 19
4. 291
5. $8.75

Lesson 117
1. 36
2. $2.50
3. 675
4. 131
5. 90

Lesson 118
1. 70
2. 30
3. 102
4. $0.75
5. 24

Lesson 119
1. 103
2. 195
3. 925
4. $5.00
5. 72

Lesson 120
1. 223
2. 100
3. 62
4. $2.79
5. 57

Lesson 121
1. 188
2. 483
3. 34
4. 278
5. 8

Lesson 122
1. 71
2. 17
3. 150
4. 311
5. 6

Lesson 123
1. 76, 72, 71, 56, 54
2. 31
3. 120
4. 612
5. bowling ball circled

Lesson 124
1. 97
2. 35, 46, 71, 88, 117
3. 110
4. 118
5. 9

Lesson 125
1. 100
2. X on 134, 48, 190
3. 77
4. 47
5. 7

Lesson 126
1. 99, 129, 216, 312, 493
2. 25
3. 6
4. 285
5. 10

Lesson 127
1. yard circled
2. 145
3. 32
4. 95
5. 7; 5; 3; 9; 2 circled

Lesson 128
1. 6
2. 431
3. 151 circled
4. 167
5. 5

Lesson 129
1. 76
2. 12
3. 59
4. 10
5. 133, 122, 115, 111, 101

Lesson 130
1. 6
2. 756 circled
3. 218
4. 173
5. 25

Lesson 131
1. 84
2. 10
3. 9
4. 58
5. 14

Lesson 132
1. 29
2. 8
3. 53
4. 616
5. 70

Lesson 133
1. 777
2. 240
3. Thursday
4. 29
5. 118

Answer Key: Lessons 134–154

Lesson 134
1. 42
2. 605
3. 182
4. 24
5. 106

Lesson 135
1. 131
2. 35
3. 311
4. 20
5. 590

Lesson 136
1. 2
2. 365
3. 220
4. 447
5. 23

Lesson 137
1. 26
2. 12
3. 33
4. 24
5. 51

Lesson 138
1. 83
2. 32
3. 19
4. 32
5. 0

Lesson 139
1. 5
2. 364
3. 65
4. 175
5. 128

Lesson 140
1. 17
2. 197
3. 360
4. 600
5. 103

Lesson 141
1. 218
2. 1,100
3. 332
4. 231
5. 8 bananas drawn

Lesson 142
1. 500
2. 222
3. 24
4. 9
5. 300

Lesson 143
1. 144
2. 209
3. 230
4. 256
5. X on 65, 43, 21, 19, 71, 49

Lesson 144
1. <
2. 103
3. square, triangle drawn
4. 40
5. 109

Lesson 145
1. 680
2. 6
3. 50
4. 6
5. =

Lesson 146
1. 90
2. 7
3. 695
4. 81
5. 9; 5

Lesson 147
1. 13
2. 700
3. 137
4. 200; 100
5. 34

Lesson 148
1. 158
2. 6
3. 329
4. 466
5. ▭▯▭▯▭▯

Lesson 149
1. 600
2. 25
3. 7
4. O
5. 38

Lesson 150
1. 7
2. 9
3. 400
4. 176
5. eraser drawn

Lesson 151
1. 46
2. 697
3. 36
4. 718
5. 207

Lesson 152
1. 43
2. 7
3. 118
4. 385
5.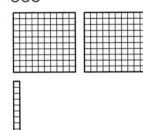

Lesson 153
1. 65
2. 110
3. 267
4. 702
5. 173 circled

Lesson 154
1. 505
2. 63
3. 43
4. 34
5. 630

Answer Key: Lessons 155–176

Lesson 155
1. 577
2. 12 circled
3. 668
4. 43
5. 154

Lesson 156
1. 41
2. 574
3. 8
4. 90
5.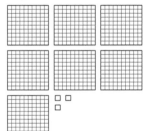

Lesson 157
1. 49
2. 6
3. 606
4. 413
5. 6

Lesson 158
1. 14
2. 58
3. 13
4. 360
5. 562

Lesson 159
1. 179
2. 400
3. 500
4. 101
5. 23

Lesson 160
1. 34
2. 4
3. 850
4. 23
5. 320

Lesson 161
1. 5
2. 88
3. 317
4. 5
5. 369

Lesson 162
1. 6
2. 234
3. 555
4. 65
5. 571

Lesson 163
1. 384
2. 225
3. 45
4. 70
5. 775

Lesson 164
1. 100
2. 229
3. 562
4. 180
5. 144

Lesson 165
1. 709
2. 84
3. 96
4. 921
5. 90

Lesson 166
1. 453
2. 87
3. 205
4. 782
5. 222

Lesson 167
1. 354
2. 218
3. 900
4. 66
5. 690

Lesson 168
1. 195
2. 12
3. 230
4. 1,003
5. 414

Lesson 169
1. 190
2. 1,000
3. 45
4. 223
5. 470

Lesson 170
1. 259
2. 17
3. 245
4. 179
5. 500

Lesson 171
1. 510
2. 790
3. 316
4. 13
5. 9

Lesson 172
1. 692
2. 267
3. 33
4. 700
5. 10

Lesson 173
1. 2 x 3 = 6 circles drawn
2. 132
3. 72
4. 4
5. circle, square drawn

Lesson 174
1. 25; 29
2. 6
3. 67
4. 51
5. 615

Lesson 175
1. 425
2. 155
3. 20
4. 190
5. star, circle drawn

Lesson 176
1. J; P
2. 55
3. 152
4. 125
5. 6

Answer Key: Lessons 177–180

Lesson 177

1. 95
2. <
3. 877
4. 8
5. 20

Lesson 178

1. 16
2. 132
3. 17
4. 305
5. 93

Lesson 179

1. 8
2. 42
3. 134
4. 156
5. 53

Lesson 180

1. 15
2. 193
3. 582
4. 109
5. 17

Assessment 1 (Lessons 1–10)

Name _____

1. 9 + 9 =

   A. 18
   B. 8
   C. 20
   D. 19

2. 8 – 7 =

   A. 1
   B. 2
   C. 14
   D. 15

3. Put the numbers in order from least to greatest.
   18, 9, 6, 20, 4.

   A. 4, 6, 9, 20, 18
   B. 20, 18, 9, 6, 4
   C. 4, 9, 6, 18, 20
   D. 4, 6, 9, 18, 20

4. Brittney orders 4 red shirts and 7 blue shirts. How many red and blue shirts does Brittney order in all?

   A. 11
   B. 3
   C. 12
   D. 10

5. Put the numbers in order from greatest to least.
   13, 3, 19, 6, 2.

   A. 2, 3, 4, 13, 19
   B. 19, 13, 3, 2, 6
   C. 19, 13, 6, 2, 3
   D. 19, 13, 6, 3, 2

6. 8 – 6 =

   A. 12
   B. 14
   C. 2
   D. 3

7. 5 + 8 =

   A. 3
   B. 13
   C. 12
   D. 15

8. What number do the Base Ten Blocks show?

   A. 18
   B. 17
   C. 20
   D. 21

Assessment 2 (Lessons 11–20)

Name _____

1. Look at the picture. Write the number sentence that the picture shows on the line.

   A. $12 + 7 = 19$
   B. $12 - 7 = 5$
   C. $12 + 8 = 20$
   D. $12 - 8 = 4$

2. $11 + 8 =$

   A. 19
   B. 18
   C. 3
   D. 21

3. $12 + 12 =$

   A. 0
   B. 25
   C. 24
   D. 18

4. Maria ran 6 miles Monday and 11 miles Tuesday. How many more miles did she run on Tuesday?

   A. 5
   B. 4
   C. 17
   D. 18

5. Choose the missing numbers to complete the pattern.
   22, 20, 18, _____, 14, _____, 10

   A. 16, 11
   B. 15, 12
   C. 16, 12
   D. 18, 12

6. $12 - 1 =$

   A. 12
   B. 11
   C. 13
   D. 10

7. $8 + \underline{\hspace{1cm}} = 10$

   A. 8
   B. 2
   C. 4
   D. 6

8. Which object or objects will complete the pattern?

   A. 2 straight lines
   B. an arrow pointing up
   C. a straight line
   D. a wavy line

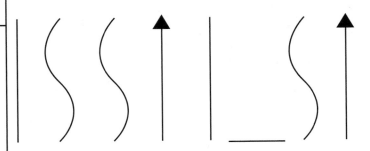

Assessment 3 (Lessons 21–30)

Name _____

1. 3 + 9 =

A. 11
B. 12
C. 6
D. 13

2. 17 – 5 =

A. 22
B. 12
C. 11
D. 10

3. 16 – 4 =

A. 13
B. 22
C. 12
D. 15

Use the bar graph to answer questions 4 and 5.

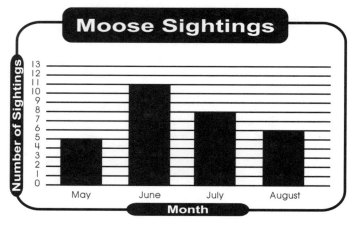

4. How many more moose were sighted during July than August?

A. 6
B. 2
C. 5
D. 4

5. How many moose sightings were there during May, July, and August?

A. 16
B. 14
C. 20
D. 19

Use the picture graph to answer question 6.

Number of Quarters Liz Spent

Monday   = 1 quarter

Wednesday

Friday

6. How many quarters did Liz spend on all 3 days combined?

A. 10
B. 9
C. 6
D. 12

7. 18 + 1 =

A. 19
B. 20
C. 18
D. 17

8. 18 + 8 =

A. 27
B. 26
C. 25
D. 10

Assessment 4 (Lessons 31–40)

Name _____

Use the picture graph to answer questions 1 and 2.

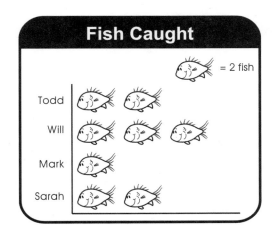

Fish Caught

🐟 = 2 fish

Todd
Will
Mark
Sarah

1. How many fish did Todd and Will catch altogether?

A. 12
B. 18
C. 10
D. 5

2. Who caught the most fish?

A. Todd
B. Will
C. Mark
D. Sarah

3. 18 – 8 =

A. 8
B. 10
C. 25
D. 26

4. 14 + 6 =

A. 8
B. 20
C. 7
D. 21

5. 17 – 2 =

A. 14   B. 15
C. 18   D. 19

6. 12 – 2 =

A. 10
B. 8
C. 14
D. 8

Use the table to answer questions 7 and 8.

Cans Collected by McGuire Family	Day	Number of Cans
	Monday	23
	Tuesday	12
	Wednesday	3
	Thursday	4
	Friday	6

7. How many more cans did the McGuire family collect on Monday than on Tuesday?

A. 10
B. 12
C. 10
D. 11

8. How many cans did the McGuire family collect in all on Wednesday, Thursday, and Friday?

A. 19
B. 18
C. 13
D. 12

Assessment 5 (Lessons 41–50)

Name _____

1. $12 + 16 =$

   A. 28
   B. 27
   C. 29
   D. 4

2. $75 + 14 =$

   A. 88
   B. 89
   C. 81
   D. 72

3. $18 - 12 =$

   A. 28
   B. 30
   C. 6
   D. 7

4. $8 + $ _____ $ = 15$

   A. 5
   B. 7
   C. 3
   D. 9

5. Marcus has 18 beads. If 12 of the beads are orange and the rest of the beads are red, how many red beads does Marcus have?

   A. 30
   B. 5
   C. 7
   D. 6

6. $24 + 24 =$

   A. 48
   B. 52
   C. 0
   D. 28

7. Which statement below best describes what is happening in the pattern?

   # 20, 15, 16, 11, 12, 7, 8, 2

   A. Five is subtracted from every number.
   B. Five is subtracted. Then, 2 is added.
   C. Five is subtracted. Then, 1 is added.
   D. Six is subtracted from each number.

8. Which answer choice will complete the pattern?

   X OO XXX X OO XXX X OO _____

   A. XXX

   B. OOO

   C. X

   D. X XX XXX

Assessment 6 (Lessons 51–60)

Name _____

1. Which symbol will make the number sentence true?

   33 _____ 13

   A. <
   B. >
   C. =

2. Round to the nearest ten. 12

   A. 20
   B. 10
   C. 15
   D. 12

3. Which number sentence does the picture show?

   A. 13 + 15 = 28
   B. 17 – 13 = 4
   C. 13 + 17 = 30
   D. 17 – 12 = 5

4. Round to the nearest ten. 45

   A. 55
   B. 45
   C. 40
   D. 50

5. Which symbol will make the number sentence true?

   15 _____ 22

   A. <
   B. >
   C. =

6. 17 + 9 =

   A. 25
   B. 26
   C. 8
   D. 9

7. 15 – 6 =

   A. 8
   B. 9
   C. 21
   D. 22

8. What is the length of the leaf?

   A. 5 meters
   B. 5 centimeters
   C. 1 decimeter
   D. 5 miles

Name _____

1. What number do the Base Ten Blocks show?

A. 60
B. 66
C. 16
D. 6

2. Which number is forty?

A. 40
B. 14
C. 44
D. 12

3. Round the number to the nearest tens place. 79

A. 70
B. 80
C. 75
D. 81

4. Which picture shows $\frac{2}{4}$ of the circles shaded?

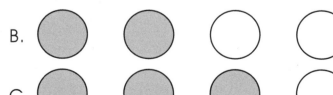

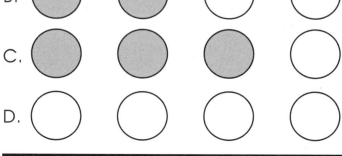

5. Which symbol will make the number sentence true?
    34 _____ 31

A. =
B. <
C. >

6. A group of 16 bees were resting on a red flower. Another 18 bees were resting on an orange flower. How many bees were resting on the red and orange flowers combined?

A. 30
B. 33
C. 34
D. 2

7. 21 − 8 =

A. 14
B. 28
C. 29
D. 13

8. Put the numbers in order from greatest to least.

    17, 18, 22, 14, 7

A. 22, 18, 17, 14, 7
B. 22, 17, 18, 14, 7
C. 7, 14, 17, 18, 22
D. 7, 17, 14, 22, 18

1. Which shape is a rectangular prism?

   A. 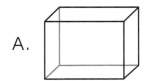 B.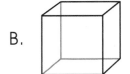

   C. D.

2. Which shape has 3 equal sides?

   A.   B.

   C.   D.

3. 42 + 84 =

   A. 125
   B. 124
   C. 126
   D. 122

4. How many corners does an octagon have?

   A. 8
   B. 6
   C. 5
   D. 4

5. 800 + 10 =

   A. 880
   B. 780
   C. 900
   D. 810

6. How many faces does a sphere have?

   A. 1
   B. 6
   C. 4
   D. 0

   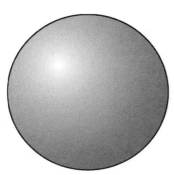

7. The second graders at Lynnwood Elementary School recycle cans. Eric brings in 29 cans on Tuesday and 18 cans on Thursday. How many more cans does Eric bring in on Tuesday than on Thursday?

   A. 10
   B. 11
   C. 17
   D. 47

8. Which block is the cat in?

   A. 2C
   B. 5E
   C. 4D
   D. 1B

   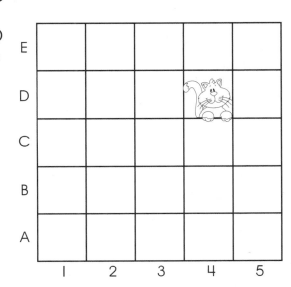

Name _____

1. Which picture shows $\frac{2}{3}$ of the apples shaded?

A.

B.

C.

D.

2. 38 + 15 =

A. 52
B. 53
C. 54
D. 23

3. 38 − 15 =

A. 53
B. 28
C. 23
D. 24

4. Estimate to the nearest tens place.

16 + 58 is about _____ .

A. 45
B. 60
C. 75
D. 80

5. Dana has 26 short-sleeved shirts and 33 long-sleeved shirts in her closet. How many short- and long-sleeved shirts does Dana have altogether?

A. 7
B. 17
C. 8
D. 59

6. Dr. Benson has 33 coffee mugs at his office. If 19 of the coffee mugs are dirty and the rest of the mugs are clean, how many clean coffee mugs does Dr. Benson have at his office?

A. 13
B. 14
C. 15
D. 52

7. 900 + 10 =

A. 880
B. 910
C. 900
D. 990

8. 80 − 60 =

A. 140
B. 30
C. 25
D. 20

Assessment 10 (Lessons 91–100)

Name _____

1. Look at the calendar. What day of the week is June twentieth?

June

Sunday	Monday	Tuesday	Wednesday	Thursday	Friday	Saturday
			1	2	3	4
5	6	7	8	9	10	11
12	13	14	15	16	17	18
19	20	21	22	23	24	25
26	27	28	29	30		

A. Sunday
B. Monday
C. Tuesday
D. Friday

2. What time is shown on the clock?

A. 8:00
B. 8:15
C. 8:30
D. 8:45

3. 558 – 18 =

A. 540
B. 475
C. 176
D. 541

4. 15 – 9 =

A. 24
B. 9
C. 6
D. 7

5. Estimate to the nearest tens place.

81 + 22 is about _____ .

A. 90
B. 60
C. 110
D. 100

6. Cynthia has 46 teddy bears in her collection. If 13 of the teddy bears are missing at least one eye, how many of the teddy bears are not missing any eyes?

A. 33
B. 34
C. 36
D. 59

7. 550 + 40 =

A. 590
B. 595
C. 485
D. 580

8. 48 – 15 =

A. 62
B. 35
C. 32
D. 33

Assessment 11 (Lessons 101–110)   Name _____

1. Susan had $0.91. She spent $0.51 at the fair. How much money does Susan have left?

   A. $1.42
   B. $1.14
   C. $1.41
   D. $0.40

2. $0.24 + $0.71 =

   A. $0.94
   B. $0.95
   C. $0.93
   D. $0.47

3. Tammy had $0.50. She earns $0.50 for helping her mother with the dishes. How much money does Tammy have now?

   A. $1.00
   B. $1.25
   C. $1.50
   D. $0.75

4. Gary has $3.50. He spends $1.00 on a snack. How much money does he have now?

   A. $2.00
   B. $3.00
   C. $2.50
   D. $4.50

5. 487 + 12 =

   A. 495
   B. 465
   C. 500
   D. 499

6. Estimate to the nearest hundreds place.

   167 + 331 is about _____ .

   A. 100
   B. 500
   C. 400
   D. 300

7. 87 − 18 =

   A. 69
   B. 68
   C. 67
   D. 65

8. 217 − 16 =

   A. 211
   B. 133
   C. 201
   D. 200

Assessment 12 (Lessons 111–120)   Name _____

1. Sarah has $4.15. She earns an additional $2.25 watering Ms. McCall's garden. How much money does Sarah have now?
    Sarah has _____ now.

    A. $6.45
    B. $6.40
    C. $6.04
    D. $2.10

2. $2.50 − $1.25 =

    A. $1.05
    B. $1.25
    C. $3.75
    D. $1.50

3. $4.50 − $2.30 =

    A. $6.80
    B. $2.25
    C. $2.20
    D. $2.05

4. Betty has $0.95 in her pocket. She loses $0.20 on her way home from school. How much money does Betty have now?

    A. $1.15
    B. $0.70
    C. $0.77
    D. $0.75

5. Patrick charges $2.25 for shoveling snow off a driveway. How much money does Patrick earn for shoveling snow off 2 driveways?

    A. $4.05
    B. $2.75
    C. $4.25
    D. $4.50

6. Estimate to the nearest dollar.

    $3.55 + $2.22 is about _____ .

    A. $5.00
    B. $6.00
    C. $7.00
    D. $4.00

7. Ellen counts 112 fish at the pet store. If 9 of the fish have stripes, how many of the fish do not have stripes?

    A. 103
    B. 100
    C. 102
    D. 110

8. 78 − 19 =

    A. 98
    B. 59
    C. 61
    D. 60

Assessment 13 (Lessons 121–130)   Name _____

1. How many blocks high is the boy?

    A. 8
    B. 7
    C. 9
    D. 12

2. How many inches long is the paintbrush?

    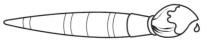

    A. 7 inches
    B. 8 inches
    C. 9 inches
    D. 10 inches

3. Put the numbers in order from least to greatest.
    255, 349, 187, 422, 411

    A. 187, 255, 349, 411, 422
    B. 411, 422, 255, 349, 187
    C. 411, 422, 349, 255, 187
    D. 187, 255, 349, 422, 411

4. Which unit is the most reasonable to measure the weight of a person?

    A. gram
    B. pound
    C. inch
    D. mile

5. How much do the tomatoes weigh?

    A. 3 pounds
    B. 4 pounds
    C. 6 pounds
    D. 2 pounds

6. 58 + 64 =

    A. 115
    B. 112
    C. 121
    D. 122

7. Isabella baby-sits 44 hours in June. In July, she baby-sits an additional 14 hours. How many hours does Isabella baby-sit in June and July combined?

    A. 58
    B. 57
    C. 60
    D. 61

8. 300 + 70 =

    A. 100
    B. 370
    C. 230
    D. 730

Assessment 14 (Lessons 131–140)

Name _____

1. If 75 of the 85 people in a restaurant order tea, how many people do not order tea?

    A. 15
    B. 14
    C. 12
    D. 10

2. 639 – 17 =

    A. 621
    B. 622
    C. 620
    D. 556

Use the bar graph to answer questions 3 and 4.

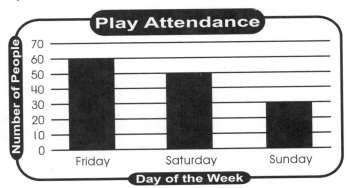

Play Attendance

3. Which night did the most people attend the play?

    A. Sunday   B. Monday
    C. Friday   D. Saturday

4. How many more people attended the play on Saturday than on Sunday?

    A. 10
    B. 30
    C. 20
    D. 0

5. 364 + 15 =

    A. 377
    B. 278
    C. 379
    D. 107

6. Look at the picture graph. How many more students did Ms. Chavez send to the computer lab on Friday than on Monday?

    A. 2   B. 15
    C. 5   D. 10

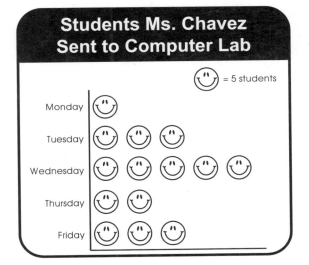

Students Ms. Chavez Sent to Computer Lab

= 5 students

7. 24 + 118 =

    A. 106
    B. 332
    C. 116
    D. 142

8. 77 – 59 =

    A. 18
    B. 19
    C. 17
    D. 136

Assessment 15 (Lessons 141–150)

Name _____

1. Choose the missing letters to complete the pattern.

   A, C, E, G, ____, K, _____

   A. I, L
   B. I, M
   C. H, M
   D. I, N

2. Choose the missing shape to complete the pattern.

   ○ ○ □ ○ ○ □ ○ __ □

   A. □

   B. ○

   C. △

   D. ▭

3. Choose the missing numbers to complete the pattern.

   50, 56, 62, ____, 74, 80, _____

   A. 68, 87
   B. 67, 85
   C. 68, 86
   D. 67, 84

4. Estimate to the nearest hundred.

   712 + 128 is about _____ .

   A. 840
   B. 900
   C. 850
   D. 800

5. Estimate to the nearest tens place.

   342 + 248 is about _____ .

   A. 600
   B. 590
   C. 580
   D. 500

6. 235 – 15 =

   A. 225
   B. 220
   C. 115
   D. 230

7. 38 – 29 =

   A. 8
   B. 12
   C. 9
   D. 67

8. 78 + 67 =

   A. 137
   B. 140
   C. 114
   D. 145

Assessment 16 (Lessons 151–160)   Name _____

1. Which number is eight hundred eleven?

A. 811
B. 801
C. 810
D. 81

2. 77 + 77 =

A. 144
B. 154
C. 115
D. 142

3. 316 + 232 =

A. 547
B. 548
C. 645
D. 149

4. What number do the Base Ten Blocks show?

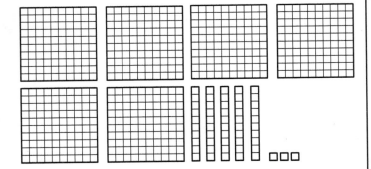

A. 536
B. 635
C. 653
D. 654

5. Margie bakes 96 cookies. She takes 59 to school to share with her class. How many cookies are left?

A. 35
B. 36
C. 37
D. 38

6. 441 – 120 =

A. 561
B. 320
C. 321
D. 560

7. What is the value of the number 8 in the number 864?

A. 8
B. 80
C. 800
D. 88

8. Which number is five hundred fifty-nine?

A. 59
B. 595
C. 509
D. 559

Assessment 17 (Lessons 161–170)   Name _____

1. 379 – 190 =	5. 567 – 433 =
A. 99 B. 189 C. 199 D. 209	A. 134 B. 135 C. 103 D. 133

2. Daniella has 113 dolls in her collection. She receives 53 more dolls for her birthday. How many dolls does Daniella have now?

A. 165
B. 166
C. 106
D. 164

6. 209 – 179 =

A. 31
B. 30
C. 35
D. 32

3. 104 + 415 =

A. 509
B. 518
C. 519
D. 591

7. 780 – 559 =

A. 219
B. 220
C. 221
D. 121

4. 200 – 187 =

A. 13
B. 27
C. 24
D. 23

8. 604 + 310 =

A. 904
B. 905
C. 914
D. 314

Assessment 18 (Lessons 171–180)   Name _____

1. Which picture below shows 3 groups of 3?

A.

B.   (three groups)

C.

D.   (three groups)

2. 784 – 599 =

A. 118
B. 105
C. 184
D. 185

3. Rachel buys 4 bags of muffins. Each bag holds 2 muffins. How many muffins are in all 4 bags total?

A. 4
B. 6
C. 8
D. 10

4. 314 + 278 =

A. 502
B. 591
C. 594
D. 592

5. 708 – 499 =

A. 209
B. 210
C. 212
D. 290

6. Mr. Andrews ordered 804 drinks and 579 pretzels for the snack bar. How many more drinks did Mr. Andrews order than pretzels?

A. 220
B. 225
C. 205
D. 383

7. 88 – 59 =

A. 27
B. 28
C. 29
D. 39

8. There are 2 lines at a store. If 3 people are in each line, how many people are in line altogether?

A. 6
B. 5
C. 7
D. 8

Assessment Answer Keys

Assessment 1
1. A
2. A
3. D
4. A
5. D
6. C
7. B
8. B

Assessment 2
1. D
2. A
3. C
4. A
5. C
6. B
7. B
8. D

Assessment 3
1. B
2. B
3. C
4. B
5. D
6. C
7. A
8. B

Assessment 4
1. C
2. B
3. B
4. B
5. B
6. A
7. D
8. C

Assessment 5
1. A
2. B
3. C
4. B
5. D
6. A
7. C
8. A

Assessment 6
1. B
2. B
3. C
4. D
5. A
6. B
7. B
8. B

Assessment 7
1. A
2. A
3. B
4. B
5. C
6. C
7. D
8. A

Assessment 8
1. A
2. B
3. C
4. A
5. D
6. D
7. B
8. C

Assessment 9
1. A
2. B
3. C
4. D
5. D
6. B
7. B
8. D

Assessment 10
1. B
2. B
3. A
4. C
5. D
6. A
7. A
8. D

Assessment 11
1. D
2. B
3. A
4. C
5. D
6. B
7. A
8. C

Assessment 12
1. B
2. B
3. C
4. D
5. D
6. B
7. A
8. B

Assessment 13
1. A
2. A
3. A
4. B
5. A
6. D
7. A
8. B

Assessment 14
1. D
2. B
3. C
4. C
5. C
6. D
7. D
8. A

Assessment 15
1. B
2. B
3. C
4. D
5. B
6. B
7. C
8. D

Assessment 16
1. A
2. B
3. B
4. C
5. C
6. C
7. C
8. D

Assessment 17
1. B
2. B
3. C
4. A
5. A
6. B
7. C
8. C

Assessment 18
1. B
2. D
3. C
4. D
5. A
6. B
7. C
8. A

Real World Application 1

Think of a number between 1 and 50. Write the number on the back of a piece of paper. On the lines below, write at least three clues about your number. Then, see if a classmate can guess the number you have described.

_____

_____

_____

_____

_____

_____

_____

Real World Application 2

Look around your classroom and find a real-life pattern. On the lines, write a sentence describing the pattern. Then, draw a picture of the pattern in the box.

_____

_____

Name _____

Real World Application 3

1. Label the 4 columns of the tally chart Dogs, Cats, Both, and Neither. Ask your classmates if they have dogs, cats, both, or neither. Record the data in the tally chart. Title your chart.

2. Use the information from the tally chart to complete the picture graph. Label and title your picture graph.

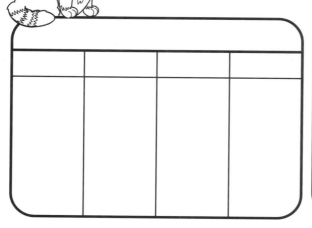

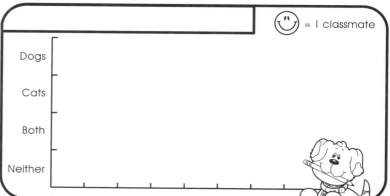

☺ = 1 classmate

Dogs

Cats

Both

Neither

Real World Application 4

1. Label the 3 columns of the tally chart Water, Soda, and Juice. Ask your classmates if they prefer water, soda, or juice. Record the data in the tally chart. Title your chart.

2. Use the information from the tally chart to complete the bar graph below. Label and title your bar graph.

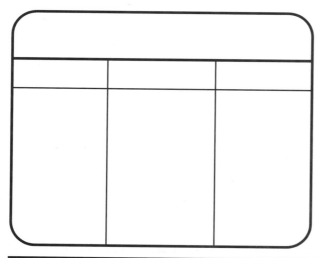

Number of Students

Water   Soda   Juice

Type of Beverage

Real World Application 5

Many quilts have patterns. An outline of a quilt is provided below. Create a pattern on the quilt. Then, on the lines below, write two complete sentences describing the pattern shown on your quilt.

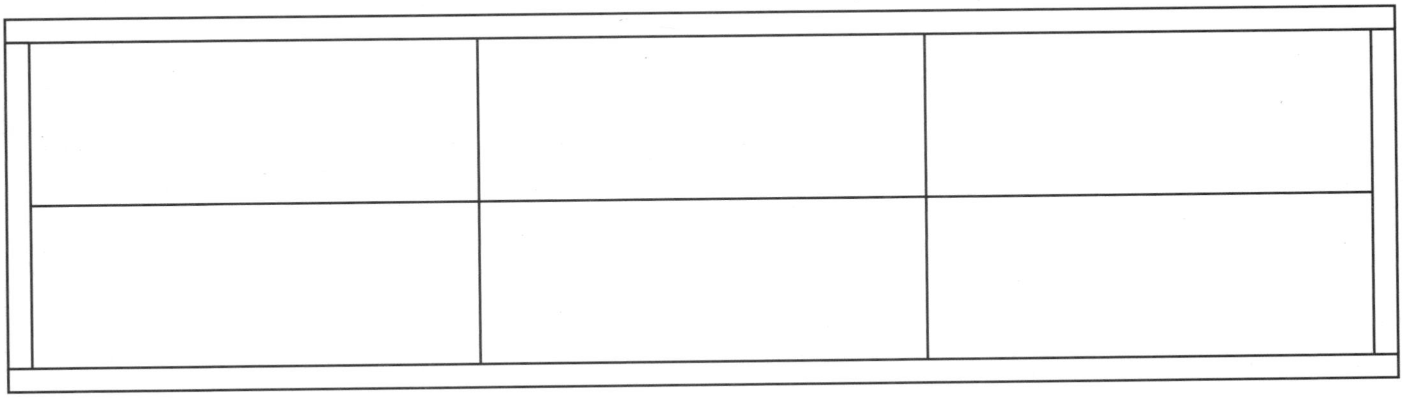

_____

_____

Real World Application 6

Look in the newspaper. Find ten places in the newspaper where a number is used. On the lines below, write about some of the important uses of numbers in our daily life and in the newspaper. Write at least three complete sentences.

_____

_____

_____

_____

_____

Real World Application 7

Fill in the calendar for this month. Write down important dates.

Real World Application 8

Make up an addition word problem and write it on the lines below. Write the answer to the word problem in the box.

_____

_____

_____

_____

_____

Real World Application 9

Make up a subtraction word problem and write it on the lines below. Write the answer to the word problem in the box.

_____

_____

_____

_____

_____

_____

Real World Application 10

In the space below, create your own repeating pattern. Leave at least two places blank in the repeated pattern. See if a classmate can figure out your pattern and fill in the blanks. If needed, give your classmate some hints about how your pattern works.

Real World Application 11

Use coin manipulatives to write your own money word problem. Then, see if a classmate can solve it.

_____
_____
_____
_____
_____
_____
_____
_____

Real World Application 12

First, use snap cubes to measure the eight objects listed below. Then, use a ruler to measure the same eight objects. Compare your answers with your classmates' answers. Discuss why your answers may or may not be different.

1. Your math book _____ snap cubes _____ inches
2. A piece of paper _____ snap cubes _____ inches
3. A book you are reading _____ snap cubes _____ inches
4. A clock _____ snap cubes _____ inches
5. A pencil _____ snap cubes _____ inches
6. An eraser _____ snap cubes _____ inches
7. A lunch box _____ snap cubes _____ inches
8. A watch _____ snap cubes _____ inches